Rosicrucian Magic, Kabbalah, and Tarot

A Guide to Rosicrucianism and Its Symbols along with Kabbalistic Tarot, Astrology, and Divination

Your Free Gift
(only available for a limited time)

Thanks for getting this book! If you want to learn more about various spirituality topics, then join Mari Silva's community and get a free guided meditation MP3 for awakening your third eye. This guided meditation mp3 is designed to open and strengthen ones third eye so you can experience a higher state of consciousness. Simply visit the link below the image to get started.

https://spiritualityspot.com/meditation

Table of Contents

Part 1: Rosicrucian Magic and Symbols

The Ultimate Guide to Rosicrucianism and Its Similarity to Occultism, Jewish Mysticism, Hermeticism, and Christian Gnosticism

Introduction

The Rosicrucians are a mystical society that has inspired fear and fascination for centuries. Most people know of the Rosicrucians through the mysterious symbolism in their secret documents.

The Rosicrucian Manifestos of the early seventeenth century describe the society as one that is part philosophical school, part scientific academy, part spiritual brotherhood, and part political party. Founded by Christian Rosenkreuz during the late fourteenth century, it was originally called the Order of the Rose Cross. It has been described as a lineage of initiates going as far back as Ancient Egypt or even Atlantis and linked to other secret societies such as Freemasonry.

This book will explore the mystery of Rosicrucianism, its symbolism, and its influence on modern secret societies. In the first chapter, we'll explain what Rosicrucianism is and give you the historical context of the society. The second chapter tells the story of Christian Rosenkreuz, the founder of Rosicrucianism. The third chapter covers the Egyptian and Hermetic origins of Rosicrucian symbolism and explains the Hermetic tradition as both a term and an esoteric system.

The fourth chapter provides a translation of an ancient Gnostic text called "Poimandres," which explains some of the symbolism of Rosicrucianism. The fifth chapter looks at the mystical Jewish tradition called Merkavah, which is closely linked to the mystery of the Holy Grail. The sixth chapter examines "Twenty-Two Paths of

Enlightenment," a system used in a few of the ancient mystic schools to train the mind.

In the seventh chapter, we look at Alchemy and Kabbalah and their relationship to Rosicrucianism. Practical aspects of Rosicrucianism, including some meditations and rituals used, are discussed in the eighth chapter. The ninth chapter covers the daily life of a Rosicrucian, or someone who practices this philosophy, and offers various tips for meditation, grounding, shielding, and other facets.

This book has two surprise bonus chapters. The first will address the sixteen Secret Signs of the Rosicrucians as they were originally composed by a medical doctor and occultist Franz Hartmann, and the other bonus chapter will explain how one goes about joining a Rosicrucian order.

The mystery of the Rosicrucian Orders has attracted the attention of many modern esotericists. They have used this symbolism in their materials, claiming that they carry on a tradition going back to the founder of Rosicrucianism, Christian Rosenkreuz. This book aims to introduce Rosicrucian philosophy and practice so that those who have no previous knowledge may find it easier to make contact with the movement. It will be helpful for occultists, students, and anyone interested in learning more about Rosicrucianism.

Chapter 1: An Introduction to Rosicrucianism

Rosicrucianism is a philosophical and religious movement that originated in early 17th century Europe. The word *Rosicrucianism* comes from the Latin "Rosae Crucis," meaning "cross of the rose." The symbol of the cross within a rose is taken from a mystic legend about Christian Rosenkreuz. They were symbolized by a circle with a cross inscribed and were worn by followers often called Magi, or wise men. Rosicrucians are distinguished from other secret societies by their emphasis on esoteric knowledge. Rosicrucianism is characterized by its interest in alchemy, mysticism, magic, and various other occult sciences.

In this chapter, the reader will find an introduction to Rosicrucianism and its history. The information provided should serve as a base for further study on the subject. Bear in mind that the scope of this chapter does not allow for a comprehensive study on Rosicrucianism. It is intended as a starting point for the reader's interest or study.

The Definition of Rosicrucianism

Rosicrucianism is a form of esoteric Christian philosophy. It is believed to have been founded in late medieval Germany by Christian Rosenkreuz. The term "Rosicrucian" describes someone associated with this philosophical and religious movement, but this does not mean that such a person is involved in all aspects. For this reason, it is true that well-known individuals such as Carl Gustav Jung and Benjamin Franklin were not members of the original order but could still be classified as Rosicrucians.

This order started with Christian Rosenkreuz, who some believe was a real historical person, but there is doubt whether he was real or allegorical. One school of thought believes he was born in 1378, lived until 1484, and was buried in a secret tomb. However, he or another Christian Rosenkreuz person may have been the mythological founder of the order or simply a symbolic figurehead.

Rosicrucianism can be considered a secret society because much of its knowledge was either privately taught to a select few or hidden in coded manuscripts. However, the idea that it is a secret society hidden from public view is a modern conception. The original Rosicrucian texts do not show an aversion to sharing their knowledge and ideas with outsiders.

The Origins of Rosicrucianism

Rosicrucians trace their origins to the early 17th century. This is due to the story that a German nobleman named Christian Rosenkreuz founded the order. According to legend, his birth had been predicted, and mysterious foster parents raised him. At the age of fifteen, Rosenkreuz began his search for wisdom, traveling to Egypt, Turkey, and Syria, and while traveling, he studied with various religious groups before finally returning to Germany. Here, he gathered a few friends who shared his interest in learning about nature and science. They decided to form an "invisible brotherhood" that would continue to seek and share their knowledge with others.

In 17th century Europe, the concept of a secret society did not have the negative connotations that it does today. However, the story of Christian Rosenkreuz and his invisible brotherhood was not well known during their time. After the publication of two anonymous manifestos in 1614 and 1615, respectively, their story gained some public attention.

These documents were the Fama Fraternitatis and the Confessio Fraternitatis, which a group of anonymous Rosicrucians published. The Fama Fraternitatis sought to establish connections between the order and other historical scholars, such as Roger Bacon. It also made claims about how Rosenkreuz and his followers used alchemy to turn base metals into gold. Finally, it stated that the Rosicrucians should be viewed as a force for good in the world.

The Confessio Fraternitatis was more of an explanatory work that sought to clarify the Fama. It also said that the Rosicrucians were interested in the study of science and religion, but not magic or sorcery.

The History of Rosicrucianism

The period of 1614 to 1616 was one of the most important in Rosicrucian history. During this time, many educated Europeans received the Fama and Confessio, which had been published as pamphlets that were widely copied and distributed. These two documents sparked a lot of interest in the Rosicrucian movement. Some of this was positive, with respected individuals such as Johannes Valentinus Andreae and Robert Fludd defending the Rosicrucians and their ideas in published works. However, others thought that the movement was a threat to Christianity and society in general.

The Rosicrucians entered a period of public silence in or around 1620, possibly due to pressure from those who saw them as a threat. After this, nothing more was published for several decades, and from 1630 to about the mid-1700s, nothing was heard from the "invisible" brotherhood either. Many assumed that the group no longer existed.

This all changed in 1710 when another manifesto was written by a Rosicrucian who called himself "Sincerus Renatus" ("The True Re-Born"). This document was entitled the Witte Opkomst ("White Flower"). In it, the author stated that he represented a German Rosicrucian lodge in Amsterdam. He sought to set the record straight about the order by clarifying its history and beliefs.

The first decades of the 18th century saw increased interest in the esoteric. This led to the publication of several Rosicrucian texts, including the 1725 Fama Fraternitatis Novi ac Vera. The author of this work, one Bernard-Matthieu Willermoz, claimed to be an initiate of the "unknown superiors" who supposedly directed the Rosicrucians. He established several secret societies in France with Rosicrucian connections, including "Les Chevaliers Bienfaisants de la Cité Sainte" (The Knights Beneficent of the Holy City) and "Les Philalèthes" (The Philalethes).

In 1767, the publication of a third manifesto generated much excitement in Masonic circles. This publication was the first document to mention Freemasonry, and claimed that both Freemasonry and Rosicrucianism were descended from a common source. It also provided new details about the original Rosicrucian brotherhood in Europe.

After that, there were no more documented communications from the invisible brotherhood. However, this did not impede the proliferation of various schools of thought that incorporated Rosicrucian concepts, including Theosophy, Anthroposophy, Spiritualism, and Rosicrucian Freemasonry. In the United States, Rosicrucian ideas have been used in several influential movements, including Transcendentalism, New Thought, and the counterculture of the 1960s.

Today there are Rosicrucian organizations in many countries around the world. While there are significant differences between them, most follow some or all of the basic concepts outlined in the Fama and Confessio Fraternitatis.

The Rosicrucian Symbol

The most recognizable symbol of Rosicrucianism is a cross surmounted by a rose. This image is also known as the Rosy Cross, Rose Cross, or Rosicrucian Cross. A symbol similar to this was also found printed in the literature of several Eastern Orthodox Christian Churches. This is a reminder of the period of history when Martin Luther and his supporters split from the Roman Catholic Church. In some European cities, including Prague, these supporters were referred to as "Rosicrucians" ("Rosy Cross") because they wore the symbol prominently displayed on their attire.

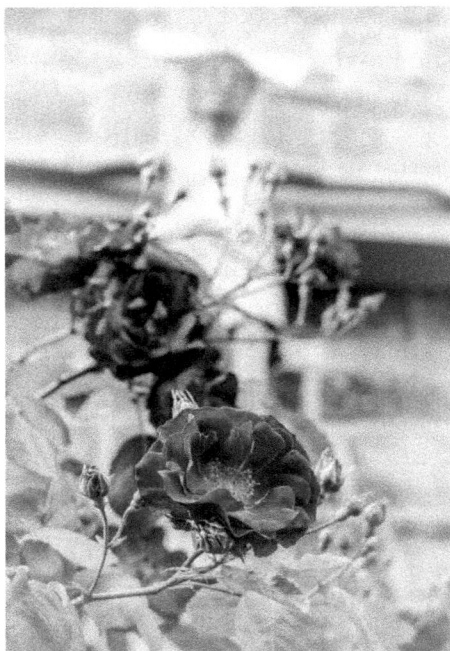

The widely accepted explanation for this symbol comes from The Chymical Wedding of Christian Rosenkreutz, a play written by Johann Valentin Andreae. In the story, Christian Rosenkreutz visits an alchemist who uses the rose and cross to represent various stages in the transformation of matter during the alchemical process. The number three is also significant because it represents material substance *and* the three divisions of the mind (thought, action, and emotion).

The rose also symbolizes spiritual love, while the cross represents moral choices. Therefore, this symbol stands for the process of attaining perfection using both mind and heart. The structure of this symbol is reminiscent of a ladder with its horizontal beam representing the physical world. This leads to an abstract representation of a three-dimensional cross. The space between the beams represents the path that is walked during the transformation process toward a state of perfection.

The alternative explanation for this symbol was written by Ferdinand Keller, one of the founders of Anthroposophy. In his essay "Die Rose-Croix," he maintains that there was an actual Rosicrucian fraternity whose symbol was a cross with roses at its ends. While this essay is considered speculative, it pointed out that the cross with a rose can be found on ancient structures throughout Europe and Asia.

Although the Rose Cross is associated with several contemporary esoteric schools of thought (such as The Golden Dawn, Thelema, OTO, Order of the Rose Cross, etc.), each one of them offers its distinctive interpretation of the symbol.

Fama Fraternitatis

The Fama Fraternitatis presents a picture of Johann Valentin Andreae as being a restless soul who wanted to promote spiritual reformation. To give credence to his aims, he invented the story of Christian Rosenkreutz and his invisible brotherhood. His purpose was not to deceive but to pique people's curiosity and lure them into wanting more information.

The Fama is divided into four parts. The first part tells of the life and death of Christian Rosenkreutz (identified as an anonymous alchemist). It also speaks about his tomb, in which are written directions for where to find documents outlining his ideas about moral conduct. Furthermore, it provides clues on how to locate this tomb (which is said to be located in the Middle East).

The second part describes the discovery of the documents left behind by Christian Rosenkreutz. Each document supposedly had a different author, but they were all written by the same person who, in the end, was revealed to be Johann Valentin Andreae himself. The documents also speak about another secret book that Rosenkreutz supposedly authored. In another one of the documents, it is written that a sect could be formed once enough people had been exposed to these ideas.

The third part tells of a different group of individuals inspired by the writings found in the tomb of Christian Rosenkreutz. They decided to form a brotherhood that promoted the ideas outlined in these documents. And they decided to call themselves "The Fraternity of the Rose Cross."

The fourth part describes how this brotherhood ended up becoming "invisible" after a rogue faction attacked it within its midst. It also warns about the dangers of pride and greed, saying that once people fall prey to these vices, they can no longer follow the path towards perfection.

Some commentators speculate that this manifesto was intended to be a literary device in which Johann Valentin Andreae could express his ideas about how society should be transformed. However, there is also historical evidence suggesting that he did sincerely believe in the existence of an actual brotherhood called the "Fraternity of the Rose Cross."

The Fraternity of the Rose Cross

The Rose Cross is an esoteric symbol that Christian Hermeticists often used. It can also be found within the writings of high-ranking clergymen, occult philosophers, and alchemists. It is often associated with the Rosicrucians due to it appearing in two works written by Johann Valentin Andreae, in which he describes the existence of the "Fraternity of the Rose Cross." The text begins with a letter from Christian Rosenkreutz, which outlines his journey to find mystical teachings in the Middle East. He also speaks about alchemy and how it can help people transform their spiritual essence.

The longer text called "Confessio" begins with Christian Rosenkreutz being brought out of the tomb he had been hidden in for 120 years. The text describes a kind of Rosicrucian manifesto about the creation and purpose of the brotherhood. It provides instructions on how to seek out hidden knowledge issued by a fraternity of "invisible brothers" who are willing to make themselves known upon reaching a certain level of awareness.

In later centuries, many occult organizations have taken on this moniker. Some of these groups are based upon the idea that Christian Rosenkreutz was an actual historical figure who played an important role in ancient mystical teachings that are currently being kept secret from most people. These groups often emulate the ideas and practices of a historical brotherhood that was supposed to have been founded during the time of Rosenkreutz.

The Rosicrucian Order Today

The Rosicrucians today claim to be carrying on the tradition of an ancient brotherhood, which Christian Rosenkreutz originally established. This brotherhood is believed to have existed for hundreds of years and reached its peak during the seventeenth century when they decided to make themselves known to other people through a series of printed documents.

Today, it is estimated that tens of thousands of individuals consider themselves to be members of this fraternity. Not all groups are the same. Some exist in groups who practice what they call "high-degree Freemasonry," while others do not require their members to go through any initiation rituals at all.

Modern Rosicrucianism is considered a very diverse group. The secret society has always been willing to accept people from all walks of life as long as they are committed to using traditional tools and techniques. Over time, these teachings have evolved into a sophisticated system, built upon the idea that certain symbols and images contain messages that are only visible to those who understand how to read them.

Today, many Rosicrucian organizations strive to emulate the original ideas of Christian Rosenkreutz by establishing secret societies capable of preserving knowledge, self-mastery, and spiritual growth. This goal, issued in the form of an ancient principle, states,

"We are all one under the sun, a solo in luce est errare," and means, *"All are one within the universe, and only by error does he err who thinks otherwise."*

It has become the principle accepted as the guiding precept by many present-day Rosicrucian groups.

Modern Rosicrucian Organization

The Rosicrucian Order is one of the largest and most well-known organizations, which claims to originate from a secret brotherhood established during the Renaissance. The group was formed in late 1909 by Harvey Spencer Lewis, who was inspired after taking part in some public exhibitions put on by an organization known as the Hermetic Order of the Golden Dawn.

Within a few years, this society had expanded throughout North America and Europe by attracting many Masons who were also interested in studying alchemy, astrology, and other forms of mysticism. They referred to themselves as an order that is *"built on esoteric truths of the ancient past."*

Today, the Rosicrucian Order has become somewhat controversial in some circles because they have been accused of being an international order of elite mystics who are trying to influence world events. The idea is that this secret society continues to flourish, despite many claims that it was shut down centuries ago when it became apparent that its goals were too ambitious.

The Order is considered to be a very secretive group, and it has not officially confirmed the idea that thousands of individuals belong to their fraternity. Many skeptics doubt whether this society meets in person or if they simply exist as an online community. Despite these claims, the Rosicrucian Order does maintain centers throughout much of North America and Europe. A General Council governs the organization, and its headquarters are located in Rosicrucian Park in San Jose, California.

It was once believed that all of the original documents which are referenced as being published by the Rosicrucian order were lost forever. After extensively studying these publications, historians have come to believe that they are not based on old manuscripts, as they first thought. Instead, all of the literature that is used by the Rosicrucian Order seems to have been written by one individual who went by the name of Max Heindel.

The development of modern Rosicrucian groups is often seen as an outgrowth from a branch known as the Rosicrucian Fellowship. This society was established in 1909 by one of its founding members, Max Heindel. In 1910, he published a book entitled The Rosicrucian Cosmo-Conception, which claimed to contain information that had been presented to him by a group of ascended masters who lived on the astral plane. The masters believed that all of this information was too advanced for most people to understand, and they only provided it to Heindel for him to disseminate it in a form that would be accessible.

The Rosicrucian Fellowship has been accused of being an elitist group because membership requires a significant donation. Critics estimate that joining the organization costs at least $27,000-$35,000. While many individuals believe this is a legitimate price for membership, others believe it is ridiculous and overpriced because this society only provides two books and a set of lectures that can be obtained through other means. The Rosicrucian Fellowship holds its meetings in a building that they refer to as the Lodge.

In 1910, Heindel also founded a magazine titled The Rosicrucian Cosmo-Conception. This publication included extensive information about spiritual practices. It could be considered one of the first modern self-help books based on esoteric principles instead of drawing information from mainstream science. This publication was eventually renamed The Rosicrucian Forum, and it continues to be published by the Rosicrucian Fellowship.

Theosophy is a religious movement that can trace its origins back to ancient times when it was believed secret knowledge could only be communicated directly from God to his chosen prophets. Today, many modern groups claim to be affiliated with Rosicrucianism, and all of them believe that they are working toward a better world by teaching individuals how to practice self-improvement.

Rosicrucianism is a spiritual order that has its roots in the 16th century, when it was believed that this society would build a utopian world. However, it was shut down centuries ago when it became apparent that its goals were too ambitious, and individuals within the society began to lose faith in its purpose. The current modern movement of Rosicrucianism was started in the early 20th century, and it aims to educate people about spirituality and esoteric practices that can lead to a better life.

The Rosicrucian Order is closely related to the Freemasonry movement because many of its original members were believed to be involved in the craft. The Rosicrucian movement also shares ties with the Hermetic Order of the Golden Dawn, a modern occult order with many similar teachings and symbols. The Rosicrucian movement is still active today and is a private spiritual group believed to be much more open and accessible than organizations such as the Freemasons.

Chapter 2: The Story of Christian Rosenkreuz

Since Ancient Egypt, Hermetic wisdom has been sought by rulers, princes, and men from all walks of life. It is no wonder, then, that the enigmatic figure of Christian Rosenkreuz would emerge from among these men seeking to revive interest in Hermetic teachings. They are known only by the name *Christian Rosenkreuz*, which means Christian Rose Cross. Very little is known about this figure since the only sources of information about his life are the narrative accounts found in <u>The Chymical Wedding of Christian Rosenkreuz</u>, published anonymously in 1616, and the <u>Universal Reformation of the Whole Wide World</u>, published anonymously in 1618.

There is a consensus among scholars that he was probably a real person, but just as there is only speculation about his origins and travels, so too it could be said that Rosenkreuz's teachings were most likely not written by him. Given that the sources of information about Rosenkreuz were published anonymously, it is not entirely surprising that there is a certain amount of confusion about his life. This chapter will discuss the story of Christian Rosenkreuz, the society's roots in European culture and alchemy, and what his teachings may have been.

The Founder of Rosicrucianism

Rosenkreuz was the name used by Christian Rosenkreuz, a mysterious figure who is said to have lived from 1378 to 1484. Who he was and where he came from is a topic of debate since the only sources of information about his life are narrative accounts included in two books published anonymously in the early 17th century.

The Chymical Wedding of Christian Rosenkreuz, published anonymously in 1616, describes a four-day wedding in which a king and queen got married. The descriptions of the figures in this ceremony are heavily symbolic, with different characters representing different alchemical concepts. The Rosicrucian Fraternity itself is mentioned when one of the participants in the wedding ceremony asks why he has never heard anyone talk about the fraternity.

The other book is entitled Universal Reformation of the Whole Wide World, published anonymously in 1618. This book describes the Fraternity of the Rosy Cross and its efforts to reform the world. It also describes the travels of Christian Rosenkreuz, his pursuit of Hermetic wisdom in the Middle East, and his foundation of an esoteric school, which was named the Fraternity of the Rosy Cross.

Rosenkreuz's origins and travels are thus described in these two books. In the Chymical Wedding, he is said to have been born in 1378 and traveled to Damascus when he was 16 years old. He was initiated by a sage named Iban Amali, who gave him the name of Peregrinus. He later traveled to Fez in Morocco and then to Spain, where he was initiated by a sage named Daedalus.

It is uncertain whether Rosenkreuz's narrative in the Chymical Wedding is allegorical (for example, that the bride and groom represented different alchemical principles) or whether these books contain an actual account of his travels. There are, however, some elements that suggest the story is not entirely fictitious. For example, Rosenkreuz mentions horticulture and alchemy as two of the disciplines he studied, both of which were growing in popularity at that time.

It is also worth noting, while these accounts were published anonymously, that there is evidence indicating Martin Luther may have written them. Certainly, the writer of the Universal Reformation of the Whole Wide World spoke in a clear style that was similar to Luther's.

The main source of information about Rosenkreuz's life may have been a fictional account, but it can be assumed that he was a real person who founded the Rosicrucian Fraternity and that his teachings had a major impact on European culture. The two books that describe his life and travels were published anonymously, so not one word can be attributed to him. Furthermore, the Rosicrucian Fraternity did not have an organized structure or hierarchy, so Rosenkreuz himself did not have to adhere to any rules. However, he likely advocated an esoteric school similar to the one described in the works published under his name.

Christian Rosenkreuz's Background and Travels

Rosenkreuz was said to be of noble birth, with his life divided between contemplation and traveling. He was born in 1378 in the town of Damm in the German province of Misnia, or perhaps in Rosheim, Alsace. At 16 years old, he left Germany, traveling through France and Spain before crossing the Mediterranean to Jerusalem. In Syria, he spent some time studying with a sage named Iban Amali. He then traveled to Alexandria in Egypt, where he spent many years studying with another sage named Daedalus.

Rosenkreuz's travels and studies continued for many years, and his knowledge of science and medicine was said to be superior to that of most other doctors. According to the story, he finally returned to Germany. On his return, he joined up with three other like-minded people who shared his vision for a society of universal knowledge and brotherhood. After this, he founded the Fraternity of the Rosy Cross (Rose Cross), which became an organization of like-minded people dedicated to studying alchemy, medicine, and other sciences. According to the story of his life, as told in the Confessio Fraternitatis and the Fama Fraternitatis, Rosenkreuz died in 1484 at the age of 106.

The story of Christian Rosenkreuz has been the subject of much speculation throughout history. Some scholars have suggested that his life is a symbolic tale, while others believe it to be an accurate account. Still, others have claimed that it is a pagan fable, written to portray Christianity in a negative light. There have even been some who have suggested that the whole story is an elaborate hoax.

Whether Rosenkreuz was an actual person or not has been debated for hundreds of years. But his legacy is still felt today whether one believes he existed or not. The fact that his story has been told for centuries demonstrates the impact he or his ideas had on people. And, if nothing else, Rosenkreuz certainly helped shape European culture with his advocacy of esoteric knowledge.

Christian Rosenkreuz's Teachings and Works

Rosenkreuz was said to have brought back knowledge from the Holy Land, including knowledge about alchemy and life after death. He also studied with wise men in Alexandria, who were the inspiration behind him establishing a school of learning when he returned from his travels. He studied with various sages, who shared their esoteric wisdom with him throughout his travels.

After returning to Germany, Rosenkreuz began his work on the Fraternity of the Rosy Cross. He aimed to create a school of learning where people could come together and work toward the common goal of learning. He believed that this was a necessary step to advance mankind and bring about a better world. In his works, Rosenkreuz included quotations that emphasized the brotherhood of man and respect for all people.

Rosenkreuz's teachings were based on the idea that people can achieve a more advanced existence by studying and working toward advancement in all things. In his story, Rosenkreuz advocates that people should study and work to gain knowledge in many areas. His teachings also told of how "truth conquers all."

Rosenkreuz's story speaks to the idea of universal brotherhood and how knowledge is one way to bring people together. His teachings were very progressive for their time, advocating that knowledge is important and should be shared. Many of his ideas would play a role in developing Freemasonry in the following centuries.

Christian Rosenkreuz's Initiatory Journey to Jerusalem

Scholars have long debated the authenticity of Christian Rosenkreuz's story. In the Confessio Fraternitatis, Rosenkreuz claims he traveled to Jerusalem and then to Egypt, where he studied in Alexandria with wise men before returning home to Germany. His journey was said to be an initiatory one, in which he progresses through the grades of the Hermetic Mysteries.

Rosenkreuz's journey to Egypt and Jerusalem is symbolic of a spiritual journey through self-knowledge. His thesis is that truth conquers all. This includes self-knowledge, which can lead to spiritual advancement and a better understanding of the world around us. The journey to Egypt and the Middle East is symbolic of leaving one's comfort zone to progress.

Christian Rosenkreuz's Initiatory Journey to Damascus

Christian Rosenkreuz also refers to a trip to Damascus in his Confessio Fraternitatis and the Fama Fraternitatis. In this letter, he writes about spending time in the Middle East and specifically in Damascus. He refers to this as an initiatory journey as well.

While the account of such a journey is certainly fictitious, it's conceivable that Rosenkreuz was referring to a real-life excursion. It is known that Rosenkreuz traveled to the Middle East, although it is less clear whether or not he visited Damascus. Damascus and Syria were both parts of the Ottoman Empire at this time, which was under the control of the Turks. The Ottoman Empire was a center of trade and intrigue during the time that Rosenkreuz lived, which would have been conducive to his account of his travels.

In any case, Rosenkreuz's journey to Damascus again speaks of spiritual initiation and the idea that, through self-knowledge, one can achieve a higher level of understanding and knowledge. His writings speak to the idea that there is always more to learn and that we should not stop seeking knowledge.

Christian Rosenkreuz's Role in the Rosicrucian Order

According to legend, Rosenkreuz established his brotherhood in 1459 and served as its head until his death. The order's full name is often given as the "Fraternitas Rosae Crucis," and it was also known as "The Order of the Rose Cross." The brotherhood was created to foster a society of individuals who would learn from each other and advance human understanding. Rosenkreuz's role in the Rose Cross Order is symbolic of how knowledge can be used to bring people together.

Rosenkreuz wrote that he was inspired to start the order after he discovered an unnamed tomb in the desert. He believed that this tomb belonged to a great philosopher. He also claimed that he was able to obtain the philosopher's writings and translate them into German, which is how much of Rosenkreuz's teachings are usually explained.

The Rosicrucian Order was a unique group of people who sought knowledge and wisdom. It was said that its members took an oath to give up all their worldly possessions and to pursue knowledge. They had promised to apply what they learned in their studies towards helping others, both within the Order and outside it.

The Rosicrucian Order was one of the first esoteric organizations of its kind to emerge in Europe. These groups focused on the idea of seeking enlightenment and how this could be achieved. They believed this was a key point in man's development, especially during Rosenkreuz's time. He and his Order heralded a new kind of knowledge and way of thinking about the world.

Christian Rosenkreuz and the First Rosicrucian Manifesto

In addition to Christian Rosenkreuz being a key figure in the history of the Rosicrucian Order, he also has an important role in the first Rosicrucian manifesto. This document, published anonymously, talked about esotericism and the brotherhood of mystery. There has been some debate over its authorship, with some claiming that it was written by Johann Valentin Andreae, a theologian and writer of that time.

Regardless of who it was written by, this manifesto is significant because it is the first of its kind. It was a new type of document that discussed topics that had never been discussed before. It focused on these two ideas and how they related to a new kind of knowledge and a unique structure for those who sought it.

Among the works of Christian Rosenkreuz is "The Universal Reformation," which he wrote shortly before his death. It was also published anonymously, although most scholars believe Rosenkreuz himself indeed wrote it. This work discussed various aspects of society and how they could be improved, demonstrating a new kind of thinking previously unseen in Europe.

Christian Rosenkreuz's Death

Christian Rosenkreuz's death coincided with the Rosicrucian manifesto. The document discussed how Rosenkreuz knew that he was dying, which is why he chose to make this work public. He did so to provide people with the knowledge to turn them into wise men/women, such as he saw himself.

This choice is important because it illustrated the type of knowledge Rosenkreuz wanted to pass on. He poured his thoughts and ideas into this document to provide people with tools to improve their lives. His wisdom is still very much in evidence today, both by those who are members of the Rosicrucian Order and outside it.

Christian Rosenkreuz died in 1484 CE. His death is surrounded by mystery and is often only vaguely described. In his work "The Universal Reformation," he refers to himself as being ill. He also says that he does not fear his impending death but feels that it is the right time for him to pass on.

What exactly happened to Christian Rosenkreuz after he published "The Universal Reformation" remains unknown. According to some sources, his tomb was discovered in 1604 CE by a group of people who wanted to re-establish the Rosicrucian Order. The tomb was empty, and Rosenkreuz's body was never located. This is often explained by saying that he achieved immortality and transcended the boundaries of death.

The idea of searching for wisdom and knowledge can be seen in other Rosicrucian works, including the Fama Fraternitatis. This was another anonymous pamphlet, which was published in Europe not too long after the Rosicrucian manifesto. The Fama was spread around various locations through word of mouth, which allowed it to reach a large audience.

In the Fama, Rosenkreuz shared his knowledge through the character of Father C.R. He did so to provide a model for those who wished to search for knowledge and wisdom themselves. His journey reflected this and pointed people in the direction that they should take. The Fama is a prominent work of Rosicrucianism, and it still inspires people to this day.

Influences on Rosenkreuz

It is unclear exactly where the influences on Rosenkreuz come from, but there are some possibilities. Some of his ideas are similar to those found in Islamic Mysticism, which focuses on the idea that people can become wise through knowledge. The Hermetic Arts, which Rosenkreuz was very interested in, are related to Islamic Mysticism. Thus, it is likely that Rosenkreuz's ideas may have come from the Muslim world. Regardless of where his influences came from, their impact on Christian Rosenkreuz and the Rosicrucian Order cannot be ignored.

Christian Rosenkreuz was a key figure in the history of the Rosicrucian Order, and his impact can still be seen today. Many of the ideas found within the organization were first introduced by him, while others influenced his thinking. Although he wrote very little and his role in creating the Rosicrucian Order is often debated, there is no denying that Rosenkreuz was influential in the formation of the organization. His ideas are still found within Rosicrucian literature, which is why he continues to be an important figure in this society. Rosenkreuz's ideas have deeply influenced many of the books currently written by the Rosicrucian Order.

Other Rosicrucian Orders

The Rosicrucian Order expanded worldwide, with various lodges popping up in different countries. Although Christian Rosenkreuz and his ideas were influential in this expansion, other factors contributed to it. One of the influences is related to European colonialism and the desire of Europeans to explore other regions. This goal brought them into contact with various aspects of foreign cultures and influenced their views on different societies, including the Rosicrucian lodge.

Another influence on the expansion of the Rosicrucian Order can be attributed to Johann Valentin Andreae. Andreae was a prominent writer and philosopher who wrote about many topics that the people at the time were interested in, including alchemy and the Rose Cross. His works inspired people to join the Rosicrucian Order by showing them that it was a place where they could learn more about these topics. The Rosicrucians prefer to keep their structure and membership private, which makes it unclear how many members the organization has. One source states that there were about three thousand members in the 1970s, although this number may have changed since then.

As for Christian Rosenkreuz himself, he no longer appears in the literature produced by the order. The few references to him are mainly related to his role in founding the Rosicrucian Order, with little written about him after that point. This is likely because of the secretive nature of the order, which makes it difficult to discuss Rosenkreuz's life. Despite this, his impact was important enough that he continues to be a prominent figure in the Rosicrucian Order. Although he wrote very little, it is clear that his ideas influenced the organization and future generations of Rosicrucians. The ideas he introduced are still found in their literature. They will likely continue to influence future members for years to come.

The Rosicrucian Order has expanded throughout the world and continues to have a large number of members today. From its beginnings in Germany, the organization has had a history that has influenced various changes in how people view the world. The succession of its leadership and expansion can be attributed to various factors which changed the organization into what it is today.

The history of the Rosicrucian Order is a dynamic one, with many factors influencing its evolution and continuation. Christian Rosenkreuz is an extremely important figure in the history of the Rosicrucian Order, and his impact can still be seen today. Rosenkreuz's complete history is surrounded by legend. Regardless of whether the stories about his life are true, there is no denying that his impact on the Rosicrucian Order is great. In addition to establishing the lodge, he introduced many of his ideas within its teachings and influenced the literature it continues to produce. While his influence cannot be understated, many other aspects of this organization's history have helped it continue until the present day. From its inception in Germany to its expansion throughout the world, the Rosicrucian Order has a long history that is interesting to explore.

Chapter 3: The Mysteries of Hermes

The philosophy of the ancient Greeks, called Hermeticism, is one of the most elusive topics in Western history. Though modern scholars have largely ignored this tradition, it nevertheless influenced many important Western esoteric currents. The Hermetic tradition can be traced back to the Greek god of alchemy, Hermes Trismegistus (Greek for "the three times great"), who was identified with the Egyptian deity Thoth, god of wisdom and keeper of the secrets of life.

Hermes Trismegistus is featured in several ancient sources, some going back to before the Common Era. A few of these texts are considered genuinely written by followers of Hermes Trismegistus or are attributed to another ancient author who was believed to have been a Hermetic initiate. Other texts are spurious or pseudepigraphic; that means an ancient author did not write them – but they were attributed to one to enhance the text's value.

The most commonly recognized books of the Corpus Hermeticum are Asclepius, Poimandres, and The Discourse on the Eighth and Ninth. The books record Hermes Trismegistus's teachings on topics such as God, the soul, and the material world. However, it should be noted that Hermeticism is not simply defined by what Hermes Trismegistus had to say. Hermeticism is an ancient philosophy that can be found in multiple ancient sources. While these sources are not always consistent with one another, they nevertheless have a common thread.

The core of the Hermetic tradition is its focus on understanding the nature of God, the soul, and the material world. Hermeticism is therefore based on rationalism because it argues that humanity can come to an understanding of God, the soul, and other matters through knowledge. Christian Rosenkreuz's knowledge of Hermeticism is reflected in his teachings and the symbolism of the Fraternity. While Christians eagerly look for direct connections between Freemasonry and Rosicrucianism and the Hermetic tradition, such connections are somewhat difficult to identify. This chapter, therefore, first introduces Hermeticism and then discusses the relevance of Hermetic ideas to Christian Rosenkreuz.

Hermetic Definitions

The term "Hermeticism" is derived from the name of the Greek god Hermes Trismegistus, who was identified with the Egyptian deity, Thoth, in Hellenistic and Coptic Egypt. The term "Hermetically" refers to Hermetics or teachings like those of Hermes Trismegistus.

Hermes Trismegistus was the legendary author of several ancient texts, some going back to before the Common Era. Most of what we know about Hermes Trismegistus comes from the historian and philosopher Flavius Philostratus (ca. 170-243 AD). In his work Life of Apollonius, Philostratus writes about a sage called "the Egyptian," who was believed to have lived some 1,500 years before the Common Era. The sage had an incredible knowledge of history, astronomy, and mathematics and was said to be the author of more than 36,000 books (many of them on magic and medicine). According to some sources, the sage was also an alchemist who could transmute base metals into gold.

Richard Hamer calls the sage "a figure of almost unimaginable antiquity" (The Hidden Art: Alchemical and Occult Symbolism in Art [New York: Thames and Hudson, 1981]). Although there is little evidence that points to an actual individual by the name of Hermes Trismegistus, some ancient sources did believe in his existence. One reason for the historical confusion is that "Thoth" was simply one of the Egyptian forms of Hermes, which was also known as "Hermes Trismegistus" by the Greeks.

The Corpus Hermeticum

Many of the texts attributed to Hermes Trismegistus go by the name "Corpus Hermeticum," a collection containing different works. The oldest texts are believed to have been written during the first centuries AD. However, some scholars assign even earlier dates to these writings because it is doubtful whether the authors of the Corpus Hermeticum were still living at the times when their texts were attributed to them.

The exact number of books that make up the Corpus Hermeticum is not certain. The most widely recognized books within this collection are "Poemandres," "Asclepius," and "The Discourse on the Eighth and Ninth." These three works contained almost all of what ancient commentators thought was important about Hermetic philosophy. However, there are some texts that older sources attributed to Hermes Trismegistus, but which have been lost. Among these are the "Three Books of Occult Philosophy" and "The Book of Hermes," a text that contains a list of astral spirits. Regarding this latter book, Karl Luckert writes:

"In it [Hermes] describes, in detail perhaps used by Renaissance-era conjurors and magicians, how to raise spirits from the astral plane and use them for magical purposes" (Symbols of Transformation in the Late Antiquity: Mysteries of the Nag

Hammadi Scriptures [London: State University of New York Press, 1995], 236).

The Corpus Hermeticum opens with what is arguably the most important work of Hermetic philosophy, Poemandres. The other texts in this collection are usually seen as commentaries on Poemandres. The Discourse on the Eighth and Ninth is another important text within the Corpus Hermeticum that deals with man's ascent toward God. Another key text that provides an insight into esoteric Hermeticism is Asclepius. This work claims to contain the words of a spiritual being who speaks about the mysteries of creation and the secrets of man's past and those of his future. In addition, there is also a series of hymns within the Corpus Hermeticum that are attributed to Hermes Trismegistus.

Branches of Hermeticism

After Hermes Trismegistus, the next figure of importance in the history of Western occultism is Cornelius Agrippa (1486-1535 AD). Several branches of occultism draw heavily on his writings. Agrippa's philosophy combined Christian theology with magical practices and Hermetic philosophy. His three-volume work on occult science, De Occulta Philosophia Libri Tres (Three Books of Occult Philosophy), is one of the best examples of this combination in Western occultism. The book deals with topics such as magic, alchemy, astrology, and Cabala (an ancient form of Jewish mysticism).

In the early seventeenth century, several occultist schools came into being. Among these were Rosicrucianism and Freemasonry. The Rosicrucians claimed to have a secret doctrine that contained a pearl of universal wisdom. In 1614 AD, someone from Germany sent an anonymous manuscript entitled Fama Fraternitatis (The Fame of the Brotherhood of RC). The book claimed to be about a secret brotherhood that was founded by Christian Rosenkreuz. It describes what this person had seen on his travels and gives instructions about how to become a member of this mystical order.

A year later, another treatise appeared under the name Confessio Fraternitatis (Confession of the Brotherhood of RC), which was probably written to refute some aspects of the first book. It gave further information about this secret society and its founder,

Christian Rosenkreuz. In 1616 AD, a third volume appeared in Germany, entitled The Chymical Wedding of Christian Rosenkreutz (with several later editions). This volume was a fiction that had many elements in common with alchemy.

The ideas of the Rosicrucian movement spread throughout Europe. Anyone who showed an interest in esoteric disciplines had heard about this mysterious brotherhood, which claimed to possess secret knowledge related to Cabala, astrology, alchemy, and magic. Several works appeared after 1616 AD that was connected to the Rosicrucian movement. These include Chemical Pathway and The Wedding of Opposites (both 1617 AD) and Theater of Terrestrial Astronomy (1619).

At the beginning of the eighteenth century, a work entitled The Chemical Treatise or Alchemical Homilies was published anonymously in England. This was probably written by Thomas Vaughan (1621-1666 AD). He was the author of Euphrates, or The Waters of the East (published in 1650 AD), which is a work that inspired mystics for generations.

The Hermetic Order of the Golden Dawn

The works of Agrippa had a wide-ranging influence on many esoteric schools. The Hermetic Order of the Golden Dawn was one of these schools. This order was founded around 1888 AD by three Freemasons, William Wynn Westcott (1848-1925), Samuel Liddell MacGregor Mathers (1854-1918), and William Robert Woodman (1828-1891). The order's mythology was based on the legend of Christian Rosenkreuz, who was also portrayed as its founder.

The Order of the Golden Dawn is best known for its teachings about magic, which took influence from both Western and Eastern esoteric traditions. Among other things, this school taught members how to work with symbols, amulets, talismans, and the Kabbalah. These symbols were connected to a ritual magic system whose rites could be used for spiritual purification, self-knowledge, and the development of consciousness.

Membership in this order required initiation into three different grades: Neophyte (initiate), Zelator (probationer), and Philosophus (philosopher). After these three grades had been completed, members were allowed to study the Kabbalah. This was an ancient form of Jewish mysticism that was closely connected to both Hermeticism and magic.

The majority of members in this order were also Freemasons. This is understandable because Freemasonry has a tradition in Western esotericism that goes back to the Middle Ages. In Freemasonry, members adopt a system of morality based on Hermetic teachings. The influence of Freemasonry on the Golden Dawn was especially clear when it came to its use of symbols and initiation rites. Members were required to wear a specific Masonic tie to participate in meetings. The names of the different degrees in this order were also derived from Freemasonry, which gave them an alchemical significance associated with transformation.

After Mathers died, Aleister Crowley (1875-1947) became the leader for the Masonic Order (or Stella Matutina), which was a branch of this brotherhood. This order was the successor to the Golden Dawn, and Crowley developed its teachings further. He is a figure who played a major role in modern Hermeticism. Among other things, he wrote several works on magic and alchemy.

Crowley also founded another magical organization called The Argenteum Astrum (or Silver Star), which Freemasonry inspired. This order still exists today and is best known for its teachings on magic. It has several lodges in different countries worldwide, including four lodges located in New York City.

One of the most influential representatives of modern Hermeticism was Carl Gustav Jung (1875-1961). He was a Swiss psychiatrist who initially studied Freudian psychoanalysis but later became interested in subjects such as philosophy and Eastern spirituality. In particular, Jung was captivated by alchemy because of its psychological symbolism. He also compared the structure of the psyche to that of matter, which is a theme found in both Hermeticism and alchemy.

Jung is sometimes considered the father of the New Age movement because of his studies in spirituality and alternative medicine. He also had an interest in astrology, which he believed was related to alchemy. While some contemporary authors label him a mystic, Jung did not identify with this term because of its religious connotations. However, he did acknowledge that he had experienced another form of reality at the beginning of his career, which is sometimes compared to a mystical experience.

This is why Jung believed in a concept called synchronicity, which was described as "meaningful coincidences." His idea was that people are connected with the world on a deeper level than can be explained by the laws of nature. From this perspective, people and "cosmic patterns" can interact with each other even if there is no causal relationship between them.

Jung founded a psychological school called *analytical psychology*. Because of its mysticism, it has been reinterpreted as part of modern Hermeticism s. For example, Jung described his theory as an empirical science based on introspection and Buddhist teachings. In some of his works, he associated the unconscious with primordial energy called "libido," which can be related to Hermetic principles such as Prana or subtle energy from Kundalini yoga.

The Symbol of the Hermetic Traditions

The symbol of the hermetic traditions is a drawing of Hermes Trismegistus that was created by the French occultist Eliphas Levi (1810- 1875). This image depicts Hermes holding an oval scepter in his left hand. There are two serpents at the top of the drawing with their heads intertwined. The right-hand snake is often portrayed as having its tail in Hermes' hand, while the left-hand one has his mouth.

The scepter Hermes is holding represents astral light or magical energy. It can also symbolize knowledge or gnosis because it is said to have been created by the ancient Egyptian god Thoth, who was known as the god of writing, magic, and wisdom. The two serpents also represent astral light, and their heads can symbolize positive and negative energy. The left-hand serpent represents the "serpent of darkness," associated with evil in ancient Egyptian mythology.

The oval shape that Hermes is holding has a double meaning. It refers to the shape of the universe, and it is supposed to represent a "vesica piscis." This term comes from Latin and means "bladder of a fish." In medieval times, people believed this was actually what you would find in the belly of a fish after cutting it open. The vesica piscis can be used as a visual representation of the intersection between two circles, which is used as a symbol for higher planes of reality.

The drawing, by Eliphas Levi, became very popular in occult circles, and it has been used as a logo by different esoteric groups such as the Hermetic Order of the Golden Dawn or Thelema. In these settings, Hermes Trismegistus is known as the initiator of the Ancient Mysteries, who taught various esoteric doctrines to humanity. This includes alchemy or "Hermetic science," which became an important part of Hermeticism.

Hermes Trismegistus was sometimes described as a god that ruled over the ancient Egyptian civilization. However, in other instances, Hermes was described as a man who lived during the pharaonic period and who had been initiated into esoteric knowledge by the ancient Egyptians. In general, modern Hermeticism is not associated with any particular culture or religion. It has been influenced by Egyptian mythology, Greek philosophy, medieval alchemy, Renaissance magic, and 19th-century occultism.

To better understand the Hermetic tradition, it is necessary to discuss the Corpus Hermetica, which is a collection of mystical texts. This body of knowledge was attributed to Hermes Trismegistus, and it became quite popular in the Renaissance period because of its links with magic and alchemy. However, modern scholars generally agree that it had no single author and it was a collection of writings from different periods and authors. The works that are included in the Corpus Hermetica date back as far as 200 BCE, but they were probably written between the third century CE and the first half of the second century CE.

The texts that make up this body of knowledge describe Hermes Trismegistus as a wise man who was able to reveal divine truths through his writings. Some of the texts that are included in this collection include "Poimandres," which is also known as "The Vision of Hermes," and it includes the earliest Hermetic writing called the "Untitled Text." Other representative works are "Asclepius" and "The Discourse of Hermes to Tat." Some scholars also include parts of the Hermetic writings found at Nag Hammadi in this body of knowledge.

The most influential work included in the Corpus Hermetica is "Corpus Hermeticum I." This was translated into Latin by Marsalis Ficini during the Italian Renaissance, who was considered the leader of the Florentine Academy at that time. This work is considered one of the foremost examples of Renaissance thought. It includes several teachings attributed to Hermes Trismegistus. For instance, there is a discussion between Poimandres and Hermes about "the One" and its "nous," a Greek term that means "mind." Hermes also reveals the secrets of nature, creation, and human beings.

The presence of Hermetic teachings in "Corpus Hermeticum I" was influential enough to impact early modern depictions of Hermes Trismegistus. Several artists from the Renaissance period depicted him as a person wearing a turban, which is similar to how it was illustrated in Islamic art. In some cases, he has been portrayed as a sage or an angel, while other artists have depicted him holding scrolls that contain occult symbols and Hermetic teachings.

Hermeticism had a considerable impact on Renaissance magic and alchemy. For instance, alchemists used the Greek name "Hermes" as a code word for their art. They believed that his name was associated with Mercury, and they considered it to be an essential element in alchemy. Renaissance magic also borrowed several symbols from Hermetic writings and used them as part of their rituals and attempts to communicate with celestial entities.

In many cases, the Hermeticism of the Renaissance was used for political purposes. Some Italian rulers tried to legitimize their power by using occult symbols and linking them with their rule. Cosimo de Medici (1389-1464) was one of these rulers, and he became interested in Hermetic teachings due to his friendship with Ficino. Cosimo was an important patron of the Renaissance, and he also sponsored translations of Greek texts into Latin, which included Hermetic writings.

Although it is not possible to point out a single definition for Hermeticism, it can be said that this ancient tradition is associated with specific symbols, teachings, and rituals. It has influenced many occult and esoteric traditions, while its presence has also been seen in modern practices.

In summary, Hermeticism is an ancient tradition that has influenced many occult and esoteric traditions. Some of the most well-known influences it had on modern traditions include its influence on alchemy and Renaissance magic. Christian Rosenkreuz, who is the hero of the Rosicrucian Manifestos, was influenced by Hermetic teachings. He studied them during his travels, and he tried to pass some of the knowledge that he acquired onto other people. Among the knowledge he transmitted were occult teachings, which his followers believed could be used to achieve mystical goals. The Rosicrucian Manifestos also revealed several symbols which are still used today by modern Rosicrucians.

Chapter 4: Poimandres: A Gnostic Manuscript

The Hermetic writings are a collection of ancient Egyptian texts that probably originated from a priestly initiatory cult in Alexandria, Egypt, around the 2nd century CE. Only a few of the cult's documents have survived, which were found in a highly fragmentary form under the title "Hermetica" (in Greek, "of the Egyptians," hence the Egyptian provenance of these texts). Some of them were long known as "writings from the temples of Egypt" (a probable source of the name Hermes Trismegistos). A famous collection of Egyptian writings is attributed to the ancient Egyptian god, Thoth, who was also called Trismegistus (as in "Thrice Great," a typical designation for Egyptian gods). The Hermetic writings were a series of texts containing a mixture of cryptic messages about numbers and letters, as well as philosophical speculations.

However, the combination of letters and numbers was considered to be especially important. To some extent, this belief has also influenced our culture today. For example, the Kabbalah (a Jewish form of mysticism) was strongly influenced by the teachings in the Hermetic writings, which dealt with the interpretation of the letters of the Hebrew alphabet. The combination of letters and numbers was not unique to ancient Egypt or Alexandria, although it is unclear whether the Hermetic writings have a purely Egyptian origin or whether they owe some of their ideas to Gnosticism, another religious movement that originated in Alexandria.

Nonetheless, the Hermetic writings were compiled by the Greeks. Therefore, there may be some gnostic influences on these texts. This chapter will discuss a particularly famous Hermetic text that has survived in a fragmentary form. It is called Poimandres, which means "the shepherd of men." This document is of great relevance to Hermeticism because it contains many of the themes found in other Hermetic writings.

The Poimandres

A first-hand account of the first Hermetic text, the Poimandres, was written by an unknown Greek author, who saw himself as a "prophet" inspired by "God" to write this text. For that reason, he wrote in the first person singular. He introduced himself as follows:

"I, Poimandres, the mind of absolute power ... wrote this for you..."

There are several reasons to doubt the authenticity of this text. With his reference to "God" and himself as a prophet, the writer appeared to take himself very seriously. His claim that he saw Poimandres, the "first" or "the mind," in a vision may be true to some extent. However, the claim that he wrote down what he had seen immediately afterward seems implausible. The text is not written in a singular style. Furthermore, it was written in Egypt, yet the author claimed that he saw "God" in an allegorical form. This implies that the author had a very Hellenistic (Greek) view of the world, which is strange if he supposedly wrote down what he had seen in a vision immediately. Presumably, it would take at least some time to shape the vision into a coherent text.

The above-mentioned textual problems could be due to the process of "translation." The text was written in a Semitic language, which is known as Coptic. This is the latest stage of the Egyptian language. However, the text may also contain remnants of Greek. The author's reference to himself as a "prophet" and his claim that he wrote down what he had seen immediately after having a vision would be difficult to explain if the text was written in Coptic. However, it is possible that he wrote down his vision in Greek and later translated it into the Coptic tongue.

The text of the Poimandres is divided into three sections. This division was first proposed by the English mathematician and philosopher Sir Thomas Browne (1605-1682). The book is written as an apocalyptic vision of what would happen if the teachings of Poimandres were not followed. The first section concerns itself with knowledge, whereas the second and third sections focus on ethics.

The Contents of the Poimandres

The Poimandres is written in the form of a dialogue between Poimandres and Hermes Trismegistus, who is considered to be an influential figure in Hermeticism, but our knowledge of this person is severely limited. Poimandres is the teacher within this dialogue, and Hermes Trismegistus is the pupil. Poimandres even claims to have written on stone tablets, which he wants Hermes Trismegistus to read.

The Poimandres begins with describing an apocalyptic vision in which Poimandres, who represents divine wisdom, explains the origin of the universe and how everything is composed of light. This was an important theme for Hermeticists because it explained how evil could be present in everything that exists but remain concealed.

The second section of the Poimandres is also apocalyptic. Hermes Trismegistus sees visions of future events which are reminiscent of well-known wars and plagues. This section is especially important to Hermeticists because it states that the Egyptian god Thoth will bring about a spiritual renewal in the future. However, it is not clear whether this would happen through inventions or divine intervention from another world. The second section ends with Hermes Trismegistus seeing his physical body lying dead on the ground.

Hermes Trismegistus does not experience death but continues to live in the spiritual world. He sees a "palace" and is led into it by Poimandres. There, Hermes Trismegistus experienced what he described as "martyrdom." However, his physical body remained alive and healthy. The third section of the Poimandres is a highly regarded source for Hermeticists because it deals with the question of how to achieve illumination. Poimandres explains that Hermes Trismegistus must combine his reason with faith to achieve knowledge. This combination is also explained more clearly by Nicolas-Claude Fabri de Peiresc (1580-1637), a French lawyer who was an important Hermeticist in the early 17th century.

The way to achieve illumination is also explained in the second section of the Poimandres. Hermes Trismegistus must focus his attention on spiritual matters and not be distracted by material things, according to Peiresc. This process is known as "purification." However, not all scholars agree as to the exact meaning of this term. It's also possible that the two words had distinctly different meanings. Some focused on this topic more from an ethical point of view, while others wanted purity for its own sake.

Despite this, a central theme in the Poimandres is that anyone can achieve illumination. However, the way to achieve this state is always difficult and painful because it requires an inner transformation of mind and soul. This transformation leads to a new divine self that exists in harmony with the universe and its creator, whether their god is known as Poimandres or not.

The Poimandres was probably written by a man called Aurelius Polio, who was active in the 2nd century CE. However, scholars are not certain of this attribution. Another possibility is that some parts were written by a Christian scribe and that other parts were added later on. According to various scholars, the Poimandres was influenced by Antonius Diogenes' (3rd century) book of the same name. The author of this book claimed that God was a separate entity from the material world, which means it may have been one of the earliest books in history to do so.

The Poimandres also predates another prominent work in Hermetic history: Hermes Trismegistus' teachings. According to certain scholars, this may mean that the concepts found in the Poimandres were not directly influenced by Greek philosophy when they were still spread orally. However, others disagree with this analysis and claim that the Poimandres show signs of Platonism.

The Importance of the Poimandres

The Poimandres was widely read in the early centuries CE. It influenced many Hermetic philosophers by providing them with a spiritual background for their thoughts and ideas. The author of this text claimed to have written these teachings using earlier manuscripts, which may mean that many philosophers before him were also influenced by Hermes Trismegistus.

The Poimandres is one of the most important books in Hermetic history for several reasons. Firstly, it is written in an intelligible language, unlike magical texts found throughout the 2nd century that were often written in incomprehensible ciphers. Secondly, it is one of the first and most important Hermetic texts that influenced many other scholars and philosophers.

Poimandres is also significant because it gives a name to its author: Hermes Trismegistus, which means "Hermes the Thrice-Greatest." This was not just limited to this text. According to some sources, Hermes Trismegistus was an amalgamation of several Greek people who were associated with the god Hermes.

The Poimandres focuses on ascension, which is also known as "illumination" or becoming more aware of one's self and the divine world. This means that it is not just limited to Hermeticists. Anyone who is interested in seeking enlightenment can find inspiration in this text. The Poimandres is one of the oldest books that was written specifically for Hermeticists, which means that it is a crucial resource for understanding certain elements of their history and spirituality.

The Character of Poimandres

In the Poimandres, Hermes Trismegistus is taken on a journey of self-discovery by a being called Poimandres, which means "knowledge of things." This being then guides Hermes through the universe and reveals its secrets, eventually leading him to an encounter with God or the Supreme Being. Through this experience, Hermes acquires a type of divine knowledge that allows him to understand the universe and its ultimate goal.

Like many other texts in Hermetic history, including letters supposedly written by Jesus Christ or apocryphal accounts of his life, the Poimandres is full of wisdom and moral lessons, taught through a narrative about a journey. In this case, Hermes took a personalized journey leading to understanding the universe and how everything was created.

This is also one of the first books in Hermetic history where they discuss their concept of "true" or "false" gnosis, which means knowledge. According to some scholars, this means we can read the Poimandres as an esoteric guide for self-discovery, like other Gnostic scriptures found in Eastern religions. Poimandres is not the only text in Hermetic history that discusses knowledge. In fact, this idea could be traced back to the Corpus Hermeticum, which was written between the 2nd and 4th centuries CE. This means that knowledge was one of the central concepts in Hermetic history, which likely contributed to their drive for knowledge.

The Poimandres is not only an important text because it influenced other scholars; it also highlights Hermes' journey as he seeks enlightenment and understanding. It shows how Hermes left behind his materialistic life so that he could focus on self-discovery and his connection to the divine. This is why many philosophers and scholars today still read the Poimandres, and it has impacted Hermetic history in a meaningful way that continues to inspire people.

While the Poimandres is a significant text for Hermetic history, it arguably has some Gnostic elements that can be traced back to Eastern religions. Some scholars believe that the Poimandres could have been influenced by Buddhist ideas of enlightenment and ascension through meditation. This means that Hermes may have been largely inspired by Buddhism, which also emphasizes the understanding of a supreme being and a path towards enlightenment.

The Poimandres is an important text for Hermetic history because it shows how they began to discuss gnosis or knowledge, which was likely influenced by Eastern religions like Buddhism. This means that today, we can read this manuscript as an esoteric guide that leads its readers on a path toward enlightenment.

The Pomanders, which is Latinized Greek for "the shepherd of men," or, in other words, Hermes Trismegistus, is the most famous of the Hermetic texts (Deeg & van den Broek 2). An amalgamation of several Greek cultures associated with their god Hermes (Thoth in Egyptian), Hermes Trismegistus is a combination of the Greek god Hermes and the Egyptian god Thoth. According to legend, Thoth was an intelligent being who brought writing and language to humanity at a time when everything was in chaos. As a result, a cult developed around him that sought understanding of the deeper mysteries of life through knowledge and self-empowerment.

This combination of Hermes and Thoth is most commonly depicted in the Poimandres, or "The Vision of Hermes," found in a collection of Hermetic texts called the Corpus Hermetica. This text recounts how Hermes Trismegistus is taken on a spiritual journey by Poimandres, or his "inner self" (Deeg & van den Broek 10). This journey was meant to enlighten Hermes and empower him as he gained knowledge about the universe and how everything was created, and he became closer to understanding reality.

Gnosticism and the Poimandres

The meaning of the term "gnosis" is knowledge. It was mainly popularized by Plato, who used it in his famous work, The Republic (OED). Gnostic ideas were later formed around the idea of gnosis, meaning people believed they could obtain knowledge or learn about reality through understanding and reading/observing the world around them. This knowledge, however, would often come to people through divine inspiration or illumination rather than seeing reality for what it was (OED). As a result of this philosophy, gnostic texts were not meant to be read by most people because only an "enlightened" person could fully understand their meaning (Deeg & van den Broek 11).

The Poimandres also have Gnostic elements to them. In fact, some scholars believe the term "gnosis" was coined by Hermes Trismegistus (Deeg & van den Broek 3). This means that many of the ideas associated with Gnosticism can be traced back to Hermes Trismegistus. Many parts of the text reference gnostic beliefs, such as an emphasis on meditation or knowledge that can only be obtained through self-empowerment. Hermes' goal to attain enlightenment is something that the Gnostics also emphasized.

The Poimandres have many different themes associated with them, common to gnostic texts. One of these is the emphasis on knowledge and self-empowerment. Hermes began his spiritual journey after he heard a voice that told him, *"You are immortal god"* (Deeg & van den Broek 11). After this realization, he was told by Poimandres that there is a reality beyond this physical world and that people can only understand it through understanding themselves. Hermes also learned about the seven heavens, which are considered separate realities from the physical ones. When he finally returned to his body after being enlightened, he realized that most people are not able to see what he had seen because they have not been enlightened.

Another common theme in Gnostic texts is the idea of a hostile world or demiurge. Some scholars believe that this became a central theme in many other religions after Hermes Trismegistus introduced it. In the Poimandres, the demiurge is revealed to Hermes when he asks who or what created everything. He learned that there was a "lord" of all creation called Ialdabaoth, who got lonely and decided to create other beings. Because another created this god, he was not all-knowing or powerful like his creator. However, he did not want to admit this fact. Because of his pride and unwillingness to accept that there was something greater than himself, Ialdabaoth created the world. This is similar to the concept of the demiurge in gnostic texts because it highlights how evil this world is and how people should not be willing to accept it.

Though Hermes Trismegistus was known for being a Hermetic philosopher, he also had strong ties to esotericism. The Poimandres reveal many different esoteric ideas that are still believed in today. The story of Hermes' enlightenment is also an example of esotericism. Many texts written by Hermes Trismegistus focus on knowledge and esoteric ideas. Some examples include the Kybalion, which was written around 1912, and the Corpus Hermeticum, which was written in the 2nd century CE.

Hermes Trismegistus was also known for being the author of the Emerald Tablet, which was written around 40 CE. This document has been the topic of discussion among many alchemists because it discussed many different topics related to alchemy, such as the creation of the world and the philosophy of transmutation.

Poimandres: A Gnostic Manuscript explores some of the major ideas associated with Gnosticism and Hermeticism. The text is written as a dialogue between Hermes and Poimandres, who represent knowledge or wisdom. Like many gnostic texts, it emphasizes the idea that people should seek self-enlightenment and that they can only understand reality through understanding themselves.

The Poimandres have many different influences from both Hermetic and gnostic traditions. Because Hermes was known for being the founder of Hermeticism, many people associate him with this tradition. However, Hermes was also known to have strong ties with Gnosticism, which is the main influence of the Poimandres. The text was also influenced by Egyptian mythology, which can be seen throughout the story of Hermes' enlightenment. After his enlightenment, Hermes was told that he could return to the physical world and share what he had learned if he agreed to do so. However, he was not able to return the same way because he had become wiser. Instead, Hermes had to enter the world through his son, Tat.

As is obvious from the information provided above, Hermes Trismegistus and his teachings would strongly influence many different religions and cultures. His ideas can be traced throughout history as they have been adapted to fit new purposes or changes in society. For example, the Poimandres have been used as a manifesto for Chaos Magick because it discusses different ideas relevant to this form of religious belief. In addition, the Corpus Hermeticum was a key text of Renaissance Neoplatonism because it contained ideas that people wanted to read and discover. Hermes Trismegistus starts as a pagan god, but he is also the central figure in Hermetic philosophy. His ideas have influenced many different aspects of life, which is apparent in how his story has been retold so many times.

The Poimandres has been a text of interest to many different kinds of people. This is because it contains many different religious and philosophical ideas that are still relevant to many people today. Readers often find themselves asking questions after reading the Poimandres, which can be an indication of one's own spiritual beliefs.

Chapter 5: The Mysticism of Merkavah

"All mystics speak the same language, for they come from the same country." - Louis-Claude de Saint-Martin

The mysticism of Merkavah, or the mystical tradition for chanting and praising God through the vision of His Heavenly Chariot (Ikavah), is one of the oldest mystical traditions in existence. Although there were antecedents to this tradition, such as the ancient Canaanite and Israelite Merkavah (Ikavah) literature dating back to the 5th century B.C.E., it is a mystical system that developed fully-fledged mostly during the first millennium C.E. and particularly flourished in the Middle Ages, when it was picked up and practiced by most of the Christian-European mystical orders, such as the Dionysian Artificers (founded in c. 1406), Rosicrucians (founded in 1598) and Freemasonry (founded in 1717).

The tradition of Merkavah mysticism is based on the mystical revelation of the Heavenly Merkavah (the Chariot or Throne-Chariot of God) and the "Heavenly Palaces" (Hekhalot) as described in the Rabbinic literature such as the Hekhalot and Merkavah Rabbati, and the Midrash Yelamdenu. This literature was mostly based on a body of oral traditions known in the 1st-6th centuries C.E., but which were eventually committed to writing between the 8th and 12th centuries.

The mystical practice of Merkavah is grounded in the metaphysical understanding that God is revealed in the innermost chambers (Hekhalot) of the spiritual realms. The visionary mystic would center his worship and praise of God on His Throne-Chariot (Merkavah), situated in the innermost Heavenly Palace (Hekhalot), and which contains God's Glory (Kavod). Thus, the metaphysical knowledge of the mystic is summarized in the "vision of God" on His Throne-Chariot, where He reveals Himself to be both Master (Baal) and Father (Ab), as well as Holy One (Saba).

This chapter will summarize the relevant passages in the obscure Rabbinic literature that describes the metaphysical foundation of Merkavah mysticism. The mystical symbol of God's Throne-Chariot (Merkavah) will be explored in detail. This will be followed by a summary of the mystical practice of chanting and a step-by-step analysis of the Kabalistic Cross and the Middle Pillar, an exercise based on the spheres that correspond to the middle (or central) pillar of the Tree of Life.

Kabbalah's Origins

Many Western scholars often use the term "Kabbalah" to denote the entirety of Jewish mysticism, but the use of this term is rather problematic, as it limits the scope of Jewish mysticism to one specific school of thought. The term "Kabbalah" can be understood as an umbrella term that denotes all mystical traditions within Judaism, but it must be noted that this term is not used in its original sense by Rabbinic Jews or Kabbalists. Its origin comes from the Greek QBLH, which stands for "tradition," and this term was used to denote non-canonical Jewish texts that were not part of the Hebrew Bible.

The origin of the Kabbalah comes from certain ancient traditions that can be traced back to biblical times. The core foundations of Kabbalah are the ancient writings found in the Merkavah and Hekhalot literature, also called the "Hekhalot tradition" (b. Hagigah 12a). This mystical tradition was very popular among certain circles during Talmudic times, as we find many references to it in reliable sources such as Josephus (Heinrich 2012: 108).

The term "Merkavah" literally means the Chariot, and it is used to denote God's Throne-Chariot (Ikavah) as described in Ezekiel 1:4-28 and 10:9. Most of the apocalypses found in this literature relate to one or more of the following: the Throne-Chariot of God, angels, and ministering spirits, as well as visionary journeys to consult with deceased mystics. The earliest Hekhalot literature dates back to around 200 C.E. Some scholars even argue that it originated from as early as the Tannaic Era (i.e., during the time of the early Rabbinic Sages).

The rise of Jewish mysticism, or Hekhalot literature, during the medieval era is attributed to the rampant anti-Semitism that led to increased pogroms and persecution against Jews. This eventually provoked some mystics to move towards the esoteric, as they sought new ways to explore their religion without running into too much trouble with the Christian clergy. The Kabbalah was one of the mystical movements that developed during this period, and it continued to flourish throughout Europe until its decline in the 18th century.

The literature on Merkavah mysticism is so vast that it is not possible to give a complete overview of all its facets. However, Merkavah literature can be divided into two main categories: "Hekhalot literature" and "Merkavah mystics." It must also be noted that the term "Merkavah mystic" was first applied by the German scholar G. Scholem in his extensive studies on this field of Jewish mysticism.

While most scholars agree that Merkavah literature is a clear antecedent to Kabbalistic practices, they also admit that it is not easy to pinpoint the exact origins of Kabbalah. It is "impossible to say anything definite about the origin of kabbalistic teaching" (Scholem 1969: 202). The earliest origins of Kabbalah can be traced back to the 1st century B.C.E. when Jewish mystics were inspired by non-Jewish traditions and *"by the ancient Jewish views of God and His relation to the world"* (Scholem 1974: 3).

After decades of careful study, Gershom Scholem finally concluded that the mystical movement called Kabbalah had two main sources; Merkavah mysticism and Hekhalot literature. The latter term is an abbreviation of "Hekhalot rabbati" (the greater palaces), which is the term used to denote the sevenfold heavenly halls or palaces mentioned in Ezekiel chapters 1-2. This literature forms the core of Kabbalistic mysticism, with its focus on mystical prayer and ecstatic visions.

As already mentioned, the earliest sources of Merkavah mysticism date back to around 200 C.E., when all four Gospels were written. It is also evident that various points in Ezekiel's visions (particularly Ezek. 1; 10) inspired Jewish mystics in the centuries that followed, especially when these mystics contemplated new ways to interpret sacred scripture.

How Merkavah Flourished

The literature on Merkavah mysticism flourished during the medieval era. Some of its major works were written in Spain and Provence. Perhaps one of the most influential texts was the Sefer ha-Bahir, which was so significant for Jewish mysticism that it was believed to have been "received" by the author Nechunia ben Ha-Kanah. Scholem dates its composition to between 1150 and 1225, though he notes that it is somewhat difficult to establish an accurate date for this type of literature.

The Bahir is one of the earliest texts to talk about reincarnation, which it discusses in sections 83-85. It uses the same phrase as Ezekiel's Merkavah mysticism ('the likeness of a throne) when referring to God's throne. Another significant text was Sefer ha-Temunah, which has been dated between 1185 and 1250. This text explains the concept of "exile within God" (galut panuy Elohim) by discussing the 10 divine powers (sephirot), also known as attributes, which are mentioned throughout Ezekiel's Merkavah mysticism.

Zohar's goal is to show how the mystical interpretation of the Bible establishes a special relationship between God and man. This is done by knowing God through His 10 attributes (sephirot), which were passed down to the man at the time of Creation. It also provides

"a panorama of the whole history of the world and a description of all the events which will take place from Creation to the end of days" (Scholem 1969: 243).

Kabbalah and the Occult

After Scholem's extensive research, it is clear that there are many different types of Kabbalistic mysticism. He suggests that the various approaches found in Merkavah and Hekhalot literature are finally reduced to two main types. The first of these is quoted as:

"...the attempt to unite with God himself, which is achieved through some form of merging with him, either by being completely absorbed into his being or absorbing his divine power."

The second type, which is much more common in the Zohar and later Kabbalistic works, involves the use of meditative techniques such as "prayer, asceticism, and magic." These techniques gave rise to the Kabbalistic concept of "the ascent on high" (shelf), which is also referred to as "The Great Way" or the way of perfection.

Both approaches aim to seek God through his attributes, which serve as a means of knowing Him. But they both go beyond this by encouraging practitioners to attain an even greater knowledge of these divine attributes, which can then lead to the divulging of spiritual secrets. These secrets are thought to be so powerful that they can be passed on to others for their spiritual advancement.

Particularly interesting is the fact that Merkavah mystics often spoke in veiled language, or secret code, about what they were discussing. Many of these terms were so powerful that they could not be written down in plain text. This is because some of the early Merkavah mystics believed it would cause them harm if these secret names and phrases were exposed to the world at large.

As Scholem points out, this type of belief can also be found in the Bahir, where it is stated that:

"whoever reveals these [secrets] to his friend but does not keep them hidden will lose what he has and suffer [severe] punishment" (Scholem 1969: 252).

The Jewish mystical text known as the Zohar was written by an author believed to be called Shimon bar Yohai, who lived around the time of the destruction of the second Temple in 70 CE. The book is also known by another name, The Book of Splendour (or Radiance), and it contains many ideas from Kabbalah and Merkavah mysticism.

The Bahir and Merkavah Mysticism

Sefer ha Bahir, which is believed to have been written in the 12th century in Provence, France by Isaac the Blind, reportedly provides many important ideas about Kabbalah and Merkavah mysticism. For instance, it uses Hekhalot vocabulary when discussing the 10 sephirot and speaks of the vessels that shattered in a way that is very similar to the descriptions found in 1 Enoch of the Bible.

Both the Bahir and 1 Enoch refer to "the mystery of their breaking" (Milikowsky 2000: 110). In addition, there are other parallels between these two works, including ideas about the sephirot being *"emanations of God, intermediaries between God and Creation"* (Amzallag 2005: 402). They also seem to share the same concept of *"the mystic's quest for God"* (Amzallag 2005: 402).

In other words, both these texts contain similar mystical concepts which can be traced back to Merkavah and Hekhalot literature. This is not surprising because many scholars believe that there was a strong relationship between the authors of both works.

It has been suggested by several scholars that "the visionary and mystical Jewish Hekhalot texts have their origin in the first centuries of the Common Era" (Amzallag 2005: 401). There is also a popular belief held by many students of Kabbalistic texts that the concept of Merkavah mysticism came from the prophet Ezekiel, who is believed to have witnessed these revelations during his time in exile (Amzallag 2005: 402).

Ascetic Practices and Meditation Techniques

However, it should be mentioned that there was another form of mystical tradition that arose at this time based on ascetic practices and meditation techniques, such as fasting. This form of mysticism is sometimes referred to as introversive mysticism. On the other hand, it has been pointed out by several scholars who have studied Merkavah mysticism that there were some mystics during this time who were not strictly introversive (Amzallag 2005: 402). Instead, these mystics were often well versed in the exoteric practices of Judaism and could be described as |both introversive and extroversive" (Amzallag 2005: 403).

The Tree of Life

When it comes to the Tree of Life, which is one of the most important symbols in Kabbalah, there are many different variations of its structure. The standard version includes 10 sephirot on the top row and 8 lower sephirot (or paths) on the bottom row. However, some modern interpretations include more than 10 sephirot. According to Zohar, the Tree of Life is:

"the model for all that exists." It also states that "there are ten sides to the tree and thus ten aspects are corresponding to them; they comprise all the supernal forces."

The sephirot are also said to be represented by the 22 fundamental letters of the Hebrew alphabet, and each one of them has its own particular set of meanings.

It is believed that there are ten different types of angels, which correspond with the Tree of Life, and are known as the sephirot. Each one of these angels is believed to be made out of one type of spiritual matter, with each type representing a different attribute. The sephirots are also linked to the human body because it has been pointed out that the different parts of the body, such as the limbs, the organs, and the blood, all have different properties. Furthermore, there are also many similarities between these ten sephirot and alchemy because they both use the same Kabbalistic symbols and rely on a similar style of teaching.

The central sephirah is known as Keter, and it's said to be the beginning of all things. Furthermore, it contains within it all of the hidden paths and is also known as the crown. It is also believed that this sephirah contains all ten sephirot within the "primordial ether."

The Middle Pillar Exercise

When it comes to meditation, many different techniques are used. One of the most important ones is the Middle Pillar Exercise, which is a form of Kabbalistic meditation. It is believed to be one of the easiest techniques to do because of its simplicity. This technique also works on balancing energy to restore the body to full health and heal it of any illnesses.

Depending on the context, The Tree of Life symbolizes many different things. One of the most well-known examples is that it's seen as a representation of the integral parts of human anatomies, such as the brain, the ears, and even the body itself. However, it's also often used in Kabbalistic texts to represent a divine power that is known as "Shekinah."

When it comes to the Tree of Life and the Middle Pillar Exercise, it's clear to see that there is a definite connection. The Tree of Life contains 10 sephirot which are similar to those located within the structure of the Middle Pillar Exercise. It also contains 8 paths that are represented by different types of energy that flow through the body, just like in the exercise. When doing the Middle Pillar Exercise, a person is said to be connecting themselves with different parts of nature to restore their inner balance. This is clearly shown by the importance of the sephirot, which are all located within this central point.

It's also believed that the Tree of Life has outer and inner realms. The inner part is known as Atziluth, which represents the divine world, whereas the outer part is known as Assiyah, which represents the physical world. The middle pillar is located at the very center of the Tree of Life, which represents the balance that must be achieved between these two worlds.

The Middle Pillar Exercise is said to be one of the most important Kabbalistic exercises, not only because it involves the person physically, but it also involves them spiritually. It is said to be a form of meditation that allows a person to clear their mind and focus on the task at hand. Furthermore, it also works to balance all of the connections within each person's aura. This is because the energy within each one of their chakras becomes blocked when there is an imbalance in their overall spiritual health. This is why exercise is said to be so important. However, it should only be done by a trained practitioner who has been taught how to use this method properly.

Kabalistic Cross [to be performed before meditation exercise]

Stand with your feet together, arms at your side. Inhale and raise your arms out to the sides and up above your head. Say:

"Before me, Elohim,"

When they reach shoulder height, bring your arms down and across your chest in a straight line. Touch the middle finger of your right hand with the middle finger of your left hand. Say:

"Behind me, Adonai,"

At the hip height, bring your arms up above your head on the left side in a semi-circle. Touch your left middle finger with your right middle finger. Say:

"On my right hand, Elohim."

Again, when the arms are at shoulder height, bring them down and across your chest in a straight line. Touch the middle finger of your left hand with the middle finger of your right hand. Say:

"On my left hand, Adonai."

At the hip height, bring your arms up above your head on the right side in a semi-circle. Touch your right middle finger with your left middle finger. Say:

"Above me, Elohim."

Once again, as your arms reach shoulder height, bring your arms down and across your chest in a straight line. Touch the middle finger of your right hand with the middle three fingers of your left hand. Say:

"Beneath me, Adonai."

At the hip height, bring your arms up above your head on the left side in a semi-circle. Touch your left middle finger with your right three fingers. Say:

"Within me, Elohim."

At shoulder height, bring your arms down and across your chest in a straight line. Touch the middle finger of your left hand with the middle three fingers of your right hand. Say:

"Without me, Adonai."

As you touch each finger, visualize the appropriate sephirot and then, as you touch them with your middle fingers, see each one of those spheres glowing brilliantly.

The mysticism of Merkavah has its roots in the Jewish tradition of Kabbalah. When trying to learn more about this type of mysticism, specific exercises can be done to ensure they are correctly understood. The mysticism of Merkavah is deeply connected with the Tree of Life, which is the central point of the Tree. This figure is said to be what separates the upper world (Briah) from the lower world (Assiyah). Understanding the Tree of Life is central to truly understanding Merkavah mysticism.

Chapter 6: Twenty-Two Paths of Enlightenment

"These twenty-two letters, which are the foundation of all things, He arranged as upon a sphere with two hundred and thirty-one gates, and the sphere may be rotated forward or backward, whether for good or for evil; from the good comes true pleasure, from evil naught but torment."— Sepher Yetzirah

The Tree of Life is a fundamental concept in Kabbalah, the ancient Jewish tradition of mystical interpretation. It was developed by the Jewish mystics of the Middle Ages to describe their concept of the process through which God created the universe and humankind.

The Tree is made up of ten circles, or emanations. The first three are called the Supernal Triad and are beyond human comprehension; they are associated with God Himself. The remaining seven circles, called sephirot (singular: sephirah), represent aspects of God's interaction with creation. The sephirot are connected by twenty-two paths that are symbolized by the 22 letters of the Hebrew alphabet. A thorough understanding of these connections is essential to working with the Tree.

The Tree of Life is a system, both cosmic and mundane, describing creation's origin. It represents different divine emanations consisting of ten sephirot that are interconnected by twenty-two paths. Its origins date at least to the early centuries of the 1st millennium BCE. Students who are well versed in the mysteries of the Kabbalah use it as a guide to meditation and understanding. The sephirot are arranged in three vertical columns and a top row, with three sephirot on each column, representing the supernal realm of the divine.

Each sephirah is a divine emanation influencing the creation and corresponding to one of the ten holy numbers of the Hebrews. Also, there are twenty-two paths, of which the first is the same as the last and which represent different types of creative expression. The Tree of Life is a metaphor for the stages of creation. This chapter will give a more detailed analysis of each sephirah and the twenty-two paths while explaining their correspondences with the Hebrew letters.

Sepher Yetzirah

The Sepher Yetzirah, or "Book of Formation," is an ancient work that deals with the creation of the universe by God. It is a collection of doctrines, which was written before 70 CE, and which has been attributed to an ancient Jewish sect called the Essenes. It explains how God created the universe by combining ten sephirot, which are part of all that exists. The sephirah is part of an esoteric system that reveals the secret nature of God and creation. The twenty-two paths are the bridges between each sephirah on The Tree of Life. This is a system that can be used for contemplation and one that has been important and helpful in understanding the nature of God, the world, and humanity.

The Sepher Yetzirah names the ten sephirot as: Keter, Hokma, Binah, Hesed, Gevurah, Tiferet, Netsah, Hod, Yesod and Malkut (1). The first three are the supernal triad, the highest sephirot that are beyond comprehension. The seven lower sephirot are called the arch-angels or planetary governors and are Michael, Gabriel, Raphael, Uriel, Shabbathai, Zadkiel, and (Shemhazai). All of them were created by virtue of Keter, Hokma, and Binah. Below this triad is a second one, which is also made of three sephirot; Hesed, Gevurah, and Tiferet. These are the center of divine love and divine wisdom that correspond to the three lower sephirot.

Everything is a result of the actions of these ten sephirot, which are an extension of the divine will. As the Tree of Life is a metaphor, it reveals how God can manifest in different ways. The sephirot are also connected to the four worlds of Atzilut, Beriah, Yetzirah, and Assiyah. Each sephirah is a representation of certain characteristics and virtues.

Each stage is different in the creative process, which manifests as a human being going from the embryo in the womb to birth. Once here, they grow in stages, eventually becoming fully socialized adults in society after many years. At every stage of development, there are different needs and requirements which must be fulfilled before advancing to the next stage.

The last one in the group is Malkut or Shekhinah. It has a function in the world and represents divine mercy. Malkut means "Kingdom" and is a point of concentration at the lowest level. Certain Jewish mystics hold that it is not a sephirah but a feminine principle.

In addition, there are twenty-two paths that go from one sephirah to another, and each path is a different attribute of God. These are represented by the 22 letters of the Hebrew alphabet, which have certain meanings, connections with astrology, and special symbolic significance. The Tree of Life comprises these ten sephirot, twenty-two paths connecting them, their names, and the Hebrew alphabet.

The Tree of Life

In Kabbalistic tradition, the Tree of Life is a diagram used as a teaching tool to explain the ideas of Jewish mysticism. It consists of ten sephirot and, often, twenty-two paths that connect them. The

Tree of Life is a metaphor for the stages of creation as it consists of three vertical columns that represent different parts of creation. The first column is the World of God or Emanation. It consists of ten sephirot, which represent ten types of creation. The sephirot are divine spheres that have different aspects and attributes. Also, they connect by twenty-two paths.

The Sepher Yetzirah states that God created the universe through divine spheres (sephirot) and the connecting paths (e.g., A path will connect sephirot number one with two, etc.). The Tree of Life is a metaphor for the stages of creation. The second column is Creation or Formation. It consists of ten sephirot, which are known as numbers. The third column is Nurture or Action. It consists of the six active sephirot, representing divine forces that interact with Creation and Emanation. The top row is Divine Consciousness. It consists of one sephirah that represents the divine will and purpose.

The Tree of Life is considered to be the central metaphor in the Kabbalah. It is used as a representation of God, spiritual ascent and descent, and all reality systems. The Tree of Life is based on the Sepher Yetzirah, or "Book of Formation," which explains how God created the universe through the ten sephirot, which are part of all that exists. The sephirah is part of an esoteric system, and its symbols and correspondences are used to achieve self-knowledge and understand the mystery of God.

• First Column: Emanation

The first column of the Tree of Life is called Emanation. It is the first creation from God and consists of three sephirot: Keter or The Crown, Hokhmah or Wisdom, and Binah or Understanding. They are known as the Supernal Sephiroth and surround the invisible point of divine light called The Monad. The Monad represents the divine will and is the invisible, unmanifest divinity.

The 22nd path between Keter and Hokhmah is called the Absolute or The Abyss. It is a point at which God cannot be comprehended. Within this column, ten sephirot represent numbers, which are part of all that exists. It is called Creation or Formation and consists of ten sephirot, which are known as numbers. This column represents the World of Formation; the first three sephirot surround The Monad.

- **Second Column: Creation**

Called Nurture or Action, the second column consists of six active sephirot, which represent divine forces that interact with Creation and Emanation. They are called the six primary directions of space; center, above, below, east, west, and north. There are also two sephirot at the top and bottom of this column called Malkuth or Kingdom and Yesod or Foundation.

The 22nd path is called The Sacred or Celestial Column. It connects the first sephirah, Keter, with the last one, Malkuth.

The second column is called Nurture or Action because it provides the forces necessary to keep Creation alive and active. This column has ten sephirot that represent numbers. They are part of all that exists and are known as the World of Action; they interact with Creation and Emanation. Within this column, six active sephirot provide divine forces to keep Creation alive and active.

- **Third Column: Nurture**

The third column is Divine Consciousness. It consists of the six active sephirot, which represent divine forces that interact with Creation and Emanation. They are called the Leaders of Attributes or crown, wisdom, beauty, victory, glory, and foundation.

The 22nd path is The Abyss or Fog, and it separates the second sephirah from the third. It represents an area of confusion between two parallel realities between which we can never find a resolution.

The third column is called Divine Consciousness because it represents the World of Attributes, which consists of six active sephirot with divine forces that interact with Creation and Emanation. There are six active sephirot within this column, possessing divine forces to keep Creation alive and active. They also provide the leaders of Attributes of Creation.

Tarot and the Tree of Life

A useful meditation is achieved through tarot cards, specifically the Major Arcana since it contains twenty-two cards that can be used as archetypal symbols interpreted in the human mind as depictions of our society. The Major Arcana consists of twenty-two cards that can be linked to the twenty-two paths of the Tree of Life. Each path is attributed to a specific Major Arcanum. Each card in the Minor

Arcana is also associated with one of the twenty-two paths. The Minor Arcana consists of four suits with ten cards each for a total of forty cards.

The Twenty-Two Major Arcanum

1. The High Priest (The Magician)

The path of The High Priest begins under the lowest point of the letter Vāv, which is associated with a path beginning in the sephirah Binah or Understanding. The path ascends to Hokhmah or Wisdom. Through the sephirah Understanding, we enter into the process of receiving divine energy to create our reality. Using the combined sephirot in this path, we can bring out inner traits that can be used in our outer reality.

2. The High Priestess

This path begins in the sephirah Binah or Understanding. The path ascends to the sephirah Chokhmah or Wisdom. Since The High Priestess is associated with the path beginning in Understanding, it also represents the first step of initiation. Initiation begins from receiving to creating our reality.

3. The Empress

This path begins under the lowest point of the letter Lamed, which is associated with the path beginning in the sephirah Chokhmah or Wisdom. The path ascends to Geburah or Severity. Using this sephirah, we can manifest a vision and bring it to reality through acts of will and courage. Since The Empress is associated with the path beginning at Wisdom, it also represents the second initiation step. Initiation begins from creating our reality into bringing outer traits to develop a personal vision.

4. The Emperor

This path begins under the lowest point of the letter Geburah or Severity. The path ascends to Tiphareth or Beauty. This sephirah is called the Sun, and it represents the sun on the Earth. Its warmth enables life to flourish. It is our Sun and gives us strength and nurtures our expression into a reality that all can see. Since The Emperor is associated with the path beginning at Severity, it also represents the third step of initiation.

5. The Hierophant (The Pope)

This path begins under the lowest point of the letter Yesod, which is associated with the path beginning in Tiphareth or Beauty. The path ascends to Netzach or Victory. This sephirah can be considered the foundation of consciousness through which we can receive knowledge gained by the sephirah Hod or Splendor. It is also related to Keter or Crown, which is above it on the Tree of Life. The Hierophant represents an authority that could provide quick access into our subconscious mind.

6. The Lovers

This path begins under the lowest point of the letter Netzach or Victory. The path ascends to Tiphareth or Beauty, which is considered the Sun and represents the Sun as seen from earth. Using this sephirah, we can manifest our visions into actuality through acts of will and courage. Netzach is associated with the element of water, which represents life-force energy that begins flowing when two come together.

7. The Chariot

This path begins under the lowest point of the letter Hod or Splendor. The path ascends to Geburah or Severity. This sephirah is called the Sun, and it represents the sun as seen from earth. Through this sephirah, we can also work visualization and bring our dreams to reality through acts of will and courage.

8. Strength

This path begins under the lowest point of the letter Hod or Splendor. The path ascends to Geburah or Severity, which is related to Netzach or Victory through Keter, which is above it on the Tree of Life. The Chariot represents our life-force energy that begins as soon as the sun of our vision is lit. Strength enables us to become invincible in front of any obstacles.

9. The Hermit

This path begins under the lowest point of the letter Yesod, which is associated with Tiphareth or Beauty. The path ascends to Hod or Splendor, which is related to Geburah or Severity employing Tiphareth or Beauty, considered the Sun and represents the sun we see from earth. Using this sephirah, we can manifest our visions through acts of will and courage.

10. Wheel of Fortune

This path begins under the lowest point of Malkuth, which is considered the Kingdom and represents our physical reality. The Sun or the Tiphareth is above it on the Tree of Life. The Wheel of Fortune represents a very important turning point in life that gives us more power to manifest our vision through acts of will and courage.

11. Justice

This path begins under the lowest point of Malkuth, which is considered the Kingdom and represents our physical reality. Through this sephirah, we can make our visions into reality through our acts of will and courage. Justice enables us to judge the past, present, and future.

12. The Hanged Man

This path begins under the lowest point of Malkuth, which is considered the Kingdom and represents our physical reality. The path ascends to Yesod or Foundation, which is associated with our subconscious mind. This sephirah is called the Moon, representing the feelings and emotions we possess when gathering information from the subconscious mind.

13. Death

The path begins under the lowest point of Hod or Splendor, which is related to Tiphareth or Beauty through Malkuth or Kingdom, which is considered the physical world. Death brings transformation to our visions by destroying old forms and creating new ones to make them come into manifestation.

14. Temperance

This path begins under the lowest point of Yesod or Foundation, which is associated with Hod or Splendor using Chesed or Mercy. This sephirah can bring our visions into our reach through similar qualities of will and courage. Temperance is the art of keeping two opposing forces in balance. We must understand it because it gives us needed courage and strength.

15. The Devil

This path begins under the lowest point of Hod or Splendor, which is related to Tiphareth or Beauty through Netzach or Victory. The Devil is associated with our desire to take the easy way out and avoid necessary hardships. This path enables us to destroy our desire for easy solutions.

16. The Tower

The path begins under the lowest point of Yesod or Foundation, which is associated with Hod or Splendor through Tiphareth or Beauty. The Tower represents a sudden loss of power and resources that usually occurs in the way of life when we are making decisions that go against our true potential.

17. The Star

This path begins under the lowest point of Tiphareth or Beauty, which is considered the Sun. The path ascends to Hod or Splendor, which is related to Tiphareth or Beauty employing Yesod or Foundation, associated with our subconscious mind.

18. The Moon

This path begins under the lowest point of Yesod or Foundation, which is associated with Hod or Splendor using Hod or Splendor. The Moon represents the subconscious mind, like a great sea teeming with life and monsters. This path enables us to take control of our subconscious mind and emotions.

19. The Sun

This path begins under the lowest point of Tiphareth or Beauty, which is likened to the sun. The path ascends to Netzach or Victory, where we become stronger to make our visions manifest. The Sun represents the intellect, like a blazing fire that lights up any darkness and ignorance.

20. Judgment

This path begins under the lowest point of Yesod or Foundation, which is associated with Hod or Splendor utilizing Tiphareth or Beauty. Judgment is associated with the Judgment of the visions we have manifested and how we deal with them, which can either aid or harm us.

21. The World

This path begins under the lowest point of Netzach or Victory, which is associated with Tiphareth or Beauty employing Hod or Splendor. The World represents the material world and our desire to make it a better place for all of humanity through our actions – enriching our lives and the lives of those around us.

22. The Fool

This path begins under the lowest point of Yesod or Foundation, which is associated with Hod or Splendor through Malkuth or Kingdom. This path is related to the zodiacal sign of Sagittarius, which means the "Fool" because it is associated with our subconscious mind. The Fool represents the power of intuition, which enables us to see our visions.

The twenty-two paths of the Tree of Life are a map found in most esoteric traditions that define the path to enlightenment. This map can be found in tarot cards, which are used as archetypal symbols interpreted in our minds as depictions of our society. The Major Arcana cards depict the path to enlightenment, which are twenty-two in number. When we consciously discover this map within ourselves, we can achieve the highest form of magical consciousness, which is known as enlightenment.

Chapter 7: Alchemy and Kabbalah

Alchemy and Kabbalah have been studied by many of the greatest minds throughout history. To understand the alchemical work and its symbolism, a basic understanding of Kabbalah is required. As a spiritual discipline, Kabbalah is closely related to Alchemy, and both have been studied in tandem by many over the years. Alchemical and Kabbalistic symbols often overlap and can easily be seen as complementary to each other. The relationship between the two disciplines is rooted in Hermetic philosophy, of which Kabbalah is also a part.

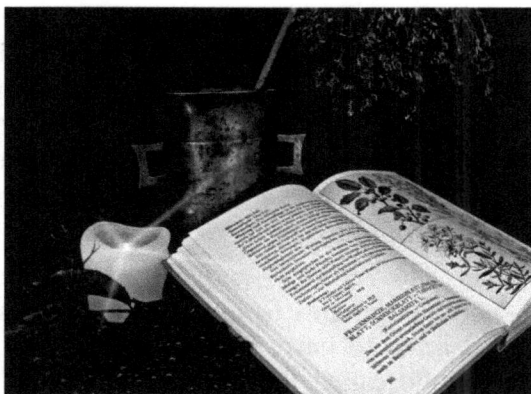

In some ways, it is easy to distinguish between Alchemy and Kabbalah. Alchemy has a long, continuous history that continues today. It is an extensive field of knowledge with many practical applications and a strong tradition of knowledge transfer. Practical alchemy is one of the root traditions in Western chemistry and industrial technology and has its roots in the medieval world. Kabbalah, on the other hand, emerged in the Jewish community at a time when Jews were persecuted almost everywhere they lived, and Kabbalistic knowledge was shared by a trusted few. For the most part, Jews were isolated from other communities, and their mystical tradition was only written down in the thirteenth century when they began to settle in Europe.

Alchemy and Kabbalah both emerged as part of the general philosophical and scientific milieu of the Middle Ages; alchemy in the twelfth century Kabbalah in the thirteenth. With its roots in ancient Egypt and Mesopotamia (roughly modern Iraq), Alchemy reached its height of popularity in Greco-Roman Egypt. Kabbalah has its roots in early Jewish mysticism and emerged in the Middle East during the early centuries of the Common Era. This chapter will first present the core concepts of Kabbalah, both linguistically and symbolically. Then it will trace the historical relationship between alchemy and Kabbalah and suggest how alchemical symbolism can be interpreted from a Kabbalistic perspective.

The Secret Doctrine

Kabbalah is part of a long tradition that includes Jewish mysticism, the mystical side of Judaism. In its written form, Kabbalistic tradition begins with the Zohar (Splendor), a thirteenth-century book written by Moses de Leon. The Zohar is considered part of the Jewish canon and is studied earnestly by traditional Jews. However, the real author of the Zohar remains a mystery, and most modern scholars doubt Moses de Leon wrote it. The Zohar is a commentary on the Torah (the five books of Moses), and most Kabbalistic literature that followed was written in this style.

Kabbalah means "to receive," and early authorities presented their teachings as direct insights from God to early Jewish mystics. Moses de Leon claimed to have received the secrets of Kabbalah from a Spanish mystic called the Rashbi. Moses de Leon's first work, Sefer Ha-Bahir (Book of Brilliance), is considered an integral part of the canon by many Kabbalist scholars/practitioners because it contains many early concepts fully developed in the Zohar.

In Jewish tradition, many of the Torah's secrets are said to have been given to Moses on Mount Sinai along with its written text. In the thirteenth century, a Spanish Kabbalist named Bahya ben Asher wrote a major work of Kabbalah called The Book of the Pious. He argued that the inner meaning of the Torah's text is as important as its material aspect. The Kabbalist cannot simply read a verse from the Bible and understand it in its simple, literal sense. It must be studied through a process that involves meditation and insight into each letter and word. This meditative approach to learning has always been part of traditional Jewish study, but Bahya ben Asher stressed its importance. He argued that the Torah comprises 613 commandments (mitzvahs). Each commandment has a literal meaning and an inner spiritual meaning, or Kabbalah.

Early Christian scholars did not share this view of the Bible's secrets. To them, the inner meaning of the text could not be reconciled with biblical inerrancy. Although they were familiar with Jewish mysticism, they generally considered it heresy and often persecuted Kabbalist Jews. And although Christian scholars studied Greek alchemy and philosophy extensively, they saw nothing of value in what they considered "Jewish magic."

The Language of Kabbalah

According to Kabbalah, the world exists because of a rupture in God's being. This idea is expressed as a linguistic paradox in its most basic form. The only way for anything to exist outside of God is for God to create it from nothing. But if something does indeed come from nothing, then how can we say that it has existence?

To discuss this paradox, Kabbalists use several different names for God. In Hebrew, these include "Ein Sof" (Without End) and "Ain" (Nothing). Using the word "nothing" to describe God is not meant to be derogatory. It reflects a deeply spiritual concept that there is no distinction between nothingness and any other kind of existence. The term "Ein Sof" is also paradoxical since it suggests that God has neither beginning nor end.

When we say that the world was created from nothing, we use the word "nothing" as if it were a substance like water or air. This idea can be understood by analogy: Imagine a cloth. If you cut a hole in this cloth, it is still the same cloth. We can ask ourselves if anything has been added or taken away from the cloth by cutting the hole. The answer is no—the hole exists within an existing whole. The "cloth" represents God in this analogy, and "the hole" represents creation.

The word "nothing" is often used in Kabbalah to describe spiritual states of being. For example, when a person becomes spiritually elevated through prayer or any other spiritual practice, the Kabbalist might say that the person has become nothing about God. Paradoxically, elevation means becoming more fully human by removing all qualities that are not God from within us. In this sense, the person has become more real and concrete about God because he no longer has a false self, or the ego, obstructing his connection with God.

Kabbalah often uses such analogies as part of its complex language. Most people find them puzzling since they go against our normal way of thinking about the world and ourselves, but Kabbalists believe that such language is necessary to reach a true understanding of God and existence.

The Symbolism of the Tree of Life

The Tree of Life is the central symbol of Kabbalah. It can be used to represent ideas and concepts and letters and words. The Tree can be drawn similarly to a grid with ten circles in its simplest form. Some of these circles are connected by lines, while others, the Sephirot (singular: Sephirah), are not connected.

Kabbalists place particular importance on the first four Sephirot: Keter (the Crown), Chokhmah (Wisdom), Binah (Understanding), and Chesed (Mercy). These are sometimes referred to as the Four Worlds since each Sephirah represents a different level of being.

Keter is pure awareness, a state in which we become aware of God within us. Chokhmah is the flash of insight that comes to us in moments of inspiration or revelation. Binah is understanding or intellectual comprehension, and it represents God's point of view. Chesed is loving-kindness and abundance, the part of God that inspires people to act with mercy. The remaining six Sephirot represent qualities associated with each level: Gevurah (Strength), Tiferet (Beauty), Netzach (Victory), Hod (Majesty), Yesod

(Foundation), and Malkuth (Kingship).

Kabbalists connect each of these attributes with the Tree's center, which represents creation. If we were to say that God is like a person, Malkuth would be the physical world and Yesod the domain of the unconscious. The Tree of Life is also important because Kabbalists use it to understand how we can transform ourselves into more spiritual beings and become one with God.

Opus Magnum

The alchemical Opus Magnum is an in-depth journey through the stages of transformation, represented by different colors. It consists of seven stages or operations; each one being associated with a spiritual state of being. The first operation is Calcination, and it represents purification. It shows that we must be purified or have our impurities removed before transforming ourselves into something more beautiful and subtle.

The second operation is Dissolution, a stage in which a solid substance is dissolved to form a liquid. In alchemy, this represents a mental and physical transformation where we can rise above the body's limitations and the ego. Separation is the third operation and symbolizes finding what is hidden or concealed within a substance and separating it from its impurities.

We reach the fourth stage, Conjunction, when we begin to transform ourselves into a new being, one that is joined with the higher order of life. We refine what we have learned from previous stages during this operation and fully understand their meaning. The fifth stage is called Fermentation, and it is compared to the miracle of bread and wine, which become a mystical substance during a religious service.

In Distillation, all impurities are removed from the substance, which has become transformed into a purer form. The final stage is called Coagulation, and it can take several forms. It represents spiritual transformation where we can transform matter into something better, just as physical food nourishes the body.

The alchemical stages of Calcination, Dissolution, Separation, Conjunction, Fermentation, Distillation, and Coagulation can also be compared to the stages of Kabbalah's spiritual path. They are not always discussed in the same order, but there is a constant return to earlier stages, so different colors often represent them. For example, the first four Sephirot are associated with the Calcination stage while Malkuth corresponds to Coagulation or Conjunction.

This alchemical process can be seen within our bodies too. Our blood circulates through the body, purifying and transforming the various substances it comes in contact with. During this purification process, impurities are removed from the organs and other parts of the body. Although we do not see it externally, we experience a transformation that eventually makes us healthier and purer inside.

The alchemists' view of the Opus Magnum (Great Work) parallels what Kabbalists describe as the process of "becoming one with God." Kabbalah and Alchemy have a great deal in common. Both traditions rely on symbols to represent ideas that cannot be described using words alone. Even though they have different origins, both traditions aim at achieving a similar goal; transforming a person and the world.

However, there are differences between Kabbalah and Alchemy. The most important difference is that alchemy deals primarily with physical matter, whereas Kabbalah is concerned with spirituality. Nevertheless, in medieval times these two subjects were studied by cultures around the world. The alchemists agreed with the Kabbalists about the importance of symbols, but they did not always agree upon what each symbol represented.

The Sacred Fire

The alchemists believed that the spirit must be released from the material elements, just as Moses lifted the serpent in the desert to free his people from physical death. The alchemists saw themselves as continuing this work of separating the pure gold of spirit from matter through their experiments with chemicals.

Since ancient times, many secret societies have performed rituals that involved raising or awakening this sacred fire, which is known as the Serpent Fire, Kundalini, or the Dragon. It is said to reside at the base of the spine within a coiled serpent. The alchemists referred to the fires of Purgatory and associated them with this physical fire that they believed was hidden in matter.

They used special substances, called quick-lime and white-fire, to help speed up the process of purification. Quick-lime is calcium oxide, which forms when you heat limestone. Alchemists use it to refer to the "heat" that helps us remove our impurities. White-fire refers to magnesium nitrate, sometimes called the spirit of nitre, which is highly combustible when combined with another substance.

Alchemists believed that the quick-lime enabled them to do their experiments because it removed all the dirt and impurities from their vessels. When quick-lime is applied to a substance, it heats up quickly and emits fumes that make it expand. This makes it a useful substance in alchemy, but if it is not used with care, the expansion can make vessels explode!

When we look at alchemical symbols, we can see what they have in common with Kabbalistic symbols. For example, alchemists used a series of pictograms that they placed in their laboratories and equipment to show which substances were inside and what their purpose was. These pictures often depicted events that were taking place at the time, and many of them refer to spiritual things.

Grounding and Centering Techniques

Grounding and centering are very useful techniques to use before performing any magical ritual. They can be used as a form of meditation or as a form of exercise to prepare your body for magical work. Raising the kundalini or awakening the serpent fire is something that has been taught in many mystery schools, including in the West.

The same thing can happen with your subconscious if you face the parts of yourself that make you uncomfortable. You can use this energy to confront your fears and learn how to become a more balanced person. Here are a couple of simple exercises that can help you do this.

Grounding Exercise 1: To Ground Is to Be Centered in the Moment

The idea behind this exercise is to bring yourself into the present moment. It is about being grounded in your surroundings which are constantly changing around you. Before performing meditation or magical work, you can use this grounding exercise since it is a good way to get into the right state of mind. However, you may find it difficult to do this exercise if you are feeling stressed or emotional.

Grounding Exercise 2: The Grounding Cord

This is a simple exercise you can use to connect yourself with the Earth. You can do it in your imagination or literally by going outside and putting a piece of string on the ground. When you go back inside, take the string with you, and keep it in a safe place until your next grounding exercise.

The visualization is as follows: Imagine yourself standing with one foot on the ground with your other leg lifted. With both hands, grab the line of string and imagine it being pulled from the ground, going up through your entire body, and sticking out of the top of your head. You can visualize a rock or some other heavy object hanging on the end of this string to bring it home. When you are ready, release your grip on the string. See it go back into the Earth and be reabsorbed by Mother Nature.

Grounding Exercise 3: A Grounding Exercise Using A Candle

This grounding exercise uses a candle flame to help you connect with your spiritual side and bring yourself into balance. You can use it to cleanse your aura and slow down the oxidation process which is going on inside your body. The exercise is as follows. Put a lit candle onto a surface and sit in front of it. Imagine a magnet sticking out of your forehead and attracting it as you stare at the flame. Float the candle in the air as if the magnet holds it. Imagine all the negative energy getting removed from your body and flying into the candle as you do this. When it is gone, you can see how your skin gains a glow, becoming more beautiful.

Advanced Middle Pillar Ritual

The Middle Pillar Ritual is a simple ritual that you can use to re-balance your energy. It helps to remove blockages in different areas of your body and helps to awaken the kundalini. When you use it with a visualization technique, you can easily increase its power because it then becomes an astral projection technique.

The ritual is performed in the following way. Firstly, you need to relax your body and try to empty your mind of all thoughts. Imagine a ball in the middle of your chest and visualize it getting bigger and bigger, filling up your entire body. When you feel fully charged, imagine that ball going into your root chakra and unleashing a wave of energy into the ground. This swirl then travels up your body, energizing all the chakras in your body. It then goes into the top of your head and down into a swirling ball that fills both your upper body and lower body. At this point, the energy passes into the earth.

You can use this ritual whenever you feel your energy is unbalanced or if you are feeling stressed out. It helps to bring yourself into the present moment, giving you the power to confront your problems.

By studying alchemy, we can get an understanding of how the alchemists saw their world. They used symbolism to represent the fire within matter and how it can be used to purify the body. By understanding this symbolism, we get a better understanding of Kabbalistic teachings, and in this chapter, we have compared a series of alchemical symbols with Kabbalistic ones to give you an insight into what these secret societies were exploring.

Chapter 8: Practical Rosicrucianism

"When the rose and the cross are united, the alchemical marriage is complete, and the drama ends. Then we wake from history and enter eternity." - Robert Anton Wilson

The Rosicrucian Order has been in existence for over four centuries, but its beliefs are not widely taught except among the more secret orders of Freemasonry. The "practical" origins of the Rosicrucians are seen in their community outreach programs through various hospitals, clinics, and institutions for those with mental illness. The Rosicrucian philosophy also theorizes that every human possesses a divine essence called the "inner god," and through meditative practices, you can not only better understand the divine but improve all aspects of life.

A Rosicrucian ritual is typically short and designed to help the participant better understand their "inner god." Through brief contemplation, certain mysteries of life are understood and practiced, such as the "mystery of the rose" and the "mystery of death." These mysteries are not necessarily unique to Rosicrucian philosophy but are concepts that have been explored by many spiritual traditions and practices. This chapter will offer an introduction to these concepts through meditation, contemplation, and other short, simple exercises.

The following are some important disclaimers to consider when practicing the exercises and rituals:

Do not perform any of these exercises/rituals if you suffer from mental illness. The reader must also stop doing any exercise if they begin to feel uncomfortable in any way. The following exercises/rituals are meant to be conducted with the guidance of an experienced Rosicrucian teacher.

Meditation on the Rose Cross Symbol to Achieve Illumination

The Rosicrucians use the rose cross symbol as an aid to meditation. When meditating on this symbol, imagine that you are looking at a flower that begins to blossom into a flower that has a stem, leaves, petals, and pistils. At the center of this plant is a cross that appears to be made of vines. Visualize the four petals on each side of the cross, having seven roses each. The cross now symbolizes resurrection. The seven roses on the cross represent the seven gifts of the Holy Spirit. These "gifts" are not considered mysterious or obscure but are considered qualities that are innate in humanity. These gifts are courage, imagination, intuition, knowledge, understanding, love, and wonder.

You can try a simple meditation on the rose cross symbol. First, sit in a comfortable seat that allows you to be both relaxed and alert. Begin breathing deeply but slowly. Imagine that you are within a rose cross, and the symbol is spinning on its axis. You can meditate on this symbol for as long as you desire. This approach aims to concentrate on your breathing, but be warned. You should only engage in activities that you feel comfortable doing.

Begin by breathing in for four counts and holding your breath for two counts. Exhale for four counts, hold your breath for two counts, and visualize a white light emerging from the crown of your head and enveloping your body. When performing this meditation, it is important to be patient and not push too hard. Simply try your best to focus and feel comfortable, and if you start to feel too uncomfortable, stop the exercise.

Meditation on Death

The Rosicrucians teach that you can truly understand death through meditation and contemplation. Many cultures throughout history have contemplated what happens after death. The Rosicrucians teach that during meditation on death, you should try to think about what you would want to be done with your dead body. You should try to imagine your own death and how those around them take the news. People commonly believe that they will go to heaven after they die, but the Rosicrucians teach that your soul is eternal and can never be destroyed.

While meditating on death, the reader may find that many difficult questions arise. Here are some common questions asked about death:

What is beyond death? What happens to our souls when we die? Where do we go when we die? Is there life after death?

While contemplating these questions, it is important to remain patient and not push too hard to find the answers. You should simply try your best to focus and feel comfortable, and again, if you feel even slightly uncomfortable, stop the exercise.

The instructions begin by suggesting that the reader considers their own death. Imagine hearing news of your own death and how you would react to it. The instructions also tell the reader to contemplate on their own soul and what happens when they die. You should imagine seeing your own body in a coffin and contemplating your next life. You can even ask yourself what you would do if you were given an opportunity to live again.

Rosicrucian philosophy teaches that it is important to contemplate death. This contemplation can be done when waking up in the morning, right before going to sleep, or at any time when you feel safe and comfortable. The meditation on death is a way of helping the reader contemplate what happens after death while also teaching them to live each day to the fullest.

During meditation, you can use various breathing techniques. For example, you can focus on slow breathing in and out in a cycle of four counts. This breathing is supposed to be done at the same pace throughout the exercise. Another technique intended to keep you calm is focusing on a white light that you envision while exhaling.

Breathing Techniques

The Rosicrucians believe that various breathing techniques can be used to calm and focus the mind. Having a calm mind is important because the mind and body are connected since your psychological state can influence your physical wellbeing. For example, breathing techniques may help lower the heart rate and blood pressure. It is also believed that breathing in certain ways helps to stimulate different parts of the brain.

1. The Fourfold Breath or Fourfold Cycle

The first breathing technique is called the fourfold breath, also known as the fourfold cycle. This technique is meant to be done slowly and evenly at the same pace throughout the exercise. It is also important to never force any type of breathing and to always breathe in and out through the nose. If you are unsure about how to perform this technique, you should consult your doctor.

For the fourfold cycle, you begin by inhaling through the nose for four counts, then exhaling for four counts, and finally inhaling again for four counts. After this cycle is complete, you should be at the point where you began. It is not necessary to count higher than four, but if you find that the breathing technique helps you stay calm and focused, you can continue to do it over a longer period of time. The reader should only use the fourfold cycle during meditation and never when feeling stressed or agitated.

2. White Light Breathing Technique

Another technique that can be used during meditation is the white light breathing technique. This technique helps the practitioner stay calm since it centers them on their breathing and encourages them to focus on the present moment rather than letting themselves get caught up in negative thinking. It is assumed that breathing in this way helps to increase energy and reduce stress.

To perform white light breathing, the reader should begin by lying down or sitting upright in a comfortable position. Take a deep breath in through the nose and imagine that you are inhaling white light. You then exhale through the mouth and see the white light traveling all around you. When beginning, you may want to focus on exhaling slowly so that it takes about four seconds to get rid of all the air in your lungs. If you find that this is too difficult, you should take smaller breaths until it becomes easier to do.

3. Lighter Breathing

The lighter breathing exercise is used to help you calm and focus your mind. It is an exercise that uses counting and movement to remain focused on the present moment. Lighter breathing is done while standing with your feet shoulder-width apart and their arms at their sides. You begin by inhaling through the nose for two counts, then exhaling for two counts. While breathing in, you should be raising your arms up to chest level, then back down to your sides again. After completing the cycle, you should be at the same point that you started at. You should continue doing lighter breathing for at least ten minutes, but if they find that it helps them stay calm and focused, they can keep doing it for longer periods.

4. Number Breath

The last breathing technique that can be used is known as the *number breath*. This exercise is meant to help quiet the mind by focusing on numbers rather than other thoughts. Any type of number can be used, but it is said that counting up to seven or higher can make someone feel anxious, so it may be best to start with one or two.

To perform the number breath technique, you should sit upright in a comfortable position with your eyes closed. Then, you should breathe in through the nose and out through the mouth for one to three counts each time. When performing the exercise, it is best to be aware of the numbers without saying them out loud. If you find that you are becoming distracted by other thoughts, you can begin to say the number in your mind, but try to concentrate on the breathing process.

The simplest method of counting is to start with one and continue to add one each time. This exercise is meant to calm you by keeping you focused on your breathing. This can be done for ten minutes or more if you feel that you need to. The most important thing is that you should not feel upset with yourself if you become distracted, but instead try to bring your mind back to the number counting.

These four breathing techniques are meant to help you reduce stress and increase your ability to remain calm. They all follow the same basic principles of focusing on breathing and not letting other thoughts enter the mind. By practicing these three or four times a day, you can start to develop a calmer and more relaxed state of mind.

White light breathing is an exercise that many people use to help themselves relax since it centers them on their breathing and encourages them to focus on the present moment. Lighter breathing is a good exercise to help the reader stay calm and focused on their body, which can be especially helpful for those who have a hard time meditating. The number breath exercise helps the reader remain focused on their breathing and not get distracted by other thoughts while also increasing their ability to remain calm. All four of these exercises are meant to help the reader reduce stress and increase their ability to stay calm by focusing on their breathing and the present moment.

Practicing Rosicrucian Rituals

Rituals can be used to help the practitioner feel calm and protected. Different types of rituals exist, such as circle casting and consecrating yourself in front of the four elements. Rosicrucian rituals are meant to be performed in the morning before starting your daily routine and at night before you go to bed. Circumstances may also dictate that the rituals be repeated throughout the day. For instance, if the person has just had their home blessed by a priest, they should do a ritual in front of the four elements so that any negative energy brought into their home will be sent back to its source. Here are some rituals that can be done when feeling emotionally or physically stressed, in front of the four elements, and consecrating yourself to the Great Work.

1. Lesser Banishing Ritual of the Pentagram

The first Rosicrucian ritual is called the Lesser Banishing Ritual of the Pentagram. It is an effective way to remove negative energy from the person's immediate surroundings and their body and persona. The ritual is meant to be done in a room or space where the practitioner feels they will not be disturbed. They should begin by standing inside a drawn circle, which will help to protect them from any negative energy they are trying to get rid of. They should then perform a scrying ritual by lighting a piece of frankincense incense and looking into the flame until they see a bright image. They should then close their eyes, put the lit incense in front of them, and focus on exhaling until they feel calm. They should then visualize breathing white light into their body through the nose before exhaling it out of the mouth.

The practitioner should then move the lit incense to their left hand and hold it close to their chest with both hands in a praying position. They should then visualize a bright pentagram painted in white light that is floating in front of them before visualizing the pentagram closing in on them like a bubble. The practitioner should then move the lit incense to their right hand and hold it close to their chest with both hands in a praying position. They should then visualize another bright pentagram painted in white light that is floating behind them before visualizing the pentagram closing in on them like a bubble.

After following these steps, the practitioner can then hold their left hand high to point upward with the palm of the hand open to the sky. They should then visualize a white pentagram painted in light above them, which will help cleanse the area of any negative energy. They should then end by holding their right hand high, pointing upwards with the palm open to the sky. They should then visualize a white pentagram painted in light below them, which will help cleanse their body and person of any negative energy.

2. Lesser Ritual of the Hexagram

The second Rosicrucian ritual is called the Lesser Ritual of the Hexagram. It is best for this type of ritual if there are four people present, one representing each element. All four people must be in good health and feel comfortable performing the ritual together. They can begin by lighting a white candle in front of each element represented in the ritual. They should then stand in the center of an equal-armed cross, with their arms in a praying position and their fingers touching in the middle. The cross represents balance and is where all four elements meet. They should then do the Lesser Banishing Ritual of the Pentagram while visualizing a bright white pentagram painted in light above and below them. Once they have done the banishing ritual, they should begin to visualize a bright white hexagram painted in light, forming an invisible barrier around them. They should then visualize a bright white pentagram painted in light above them and below them, which will help cleanse the area of any negative energy. They should then visualize a bright white hexagram painted in light inside of them that will help to keep the body healthy.

3. Rose Cross Ritual

The third Rosicrucian ritual is called the Rose Cross Ritual. This ritual aims to create an imaginary wall of protection and cleansing that can fortify our consciousness beyond the material world. It is best to do this ritual late at night in order to clear your mind of thoughts and distractions before going to sleep. The practitioner should begin by lying down in a comfortable position on their back. They should then visualize a bright white light descending from the sky and filling up their head with sacred energy. They should then visualize themselves swimming in a beautiful ocean that is filled with white light and positive energy. The practitioner should then visualize a bright white rose with 14 white petals forming out of the water and going all the way up to their head. They should then visualize a bright gold cross descending from the sky and going straight through the middle of the rose.

When they hold their right hand up high, they should visualize a bright white pentagram painted in light above them, which will help cleanse the area of any negative energy. When they hold their left hand up high, they should visualize a bright white pentagram painted in light below them, which will help cleanse their body and person of any negative energy.

These three rituals are meant to bring positive change and cleansing into your life. The Lesser Banishing Ritual of the Pentagram is a ritual meant to cleanse your living space and person. The Lesser Ritual of the Hexagram is meant to balance the energy of all elements within ourselves. The Rose Cross Ritual is meant to help create an imaginary wall of protection and cleansing.

These three rituals are all meant to cleanse yourself on a spiritual level. The purpose of cleansing yourself is so you can achieve enlightenment and be closer to God. In Kabala, the Hebrew term for God is Ein Sof, which means that nothing can exist or live outside of God. This is because words cannot describe the magnificence of God, so everything that exists is an extension of God and lives within Him. Therefore, everything that exists is God and God is everything that exists.

Rosicrucianism is a form of modern-day mysticism based on Christian Kabala and Hermeticism. It was founded by the German doctor and occultist Christian Rosenkreuz in the early 15th century. Rosicrucianism based its teachings on the study of Christian Kabala and Hermeticism. Kabala is a form of Jewish mysticism that was influenced by the Qur'an, Hinduism, and the Hebrew text, Sefer Yetzirah. Hermeticism is a system of thought influenced by the ancient Greco-Roman world's scientific and philosophical traditions.

Chapter 9: The Daily Mystic

"I will meditate on your precepts and fix my eyes on your ways." (Psalm 119:15).

The study and practice of the Rosicrucian mystical elements can bring you much closer to God than you may think. Meditation, grounding, shielding, prayer, and ritual are all vital tools in the mystic's arsenal. Rosicrucian philosophy gives insights to enlighten us in these endeavors. Daily meditation is the most important of all the mystical practices. It teaches us to avoid getting lost in our world and prevents us from being a slave to our thoughts. Grounding and shielding are great protection in our psychic battles. Prayer binds us to God and allows us to speak with Him directly. After meditation, prayer is the most important and vital tool in the mystic artist's arsenal. Ritual helps us structure our day and give meaning to each moment. This chapter will detail some of these mystical arts and how they help us on our path to God.

Meditation for Rosicrucian Mystics

The Rosicrucian philosophy is built on the foundation of meditation. This is the heart and soul of Rosicrucian mysticism. Meditation is a spiritual exercise that teaches us to become masters of our thoughts. It is the center from which all other arts and sciences are comprehended. Meditation is the entrance into mystical thinking and being, from which we can escape from our mundane lives and enter a world of infinite possibility.

The Rosicrucian daily prayer segues into meditation. Meditation is a spiritual tool that helps us keep a balance in our lives. It teaches us how to let go of the world and enter a trance-like state. It is a practical tool to help us avoid being held captive by our thoughts. Meditation is the time when we withdraw from our normal lives and enter into a new world that lies within us. It brings both time and space to a standstill, allowing us to contemplate life's great mysteries. Meditation is a two-way street providing tremendous advantages both internally and externally. It is meant to bring us closer to God.

Meditation is the key that opens the door to many other mystical avenues, including grounding, shielding, and prayer. Meditation is the heart of Rosicrucian magic and mysticism. It can help us withdraw from this world of illusions and build our inner strength. Meditation makes us strong enough to stand on our own two feet but still encourages us to look up at the stars.

Meditation is a wonderful exercise that mystics, saints, and sages have used throughout the centuries to achieve higher states of consciousness. Many people let their minds run wild with never-ending thoughts. These endless thoughts can become a heavy burden and lead to mental illness, depression, and even suicide. Meditation teaches us how to bring order into our thinking. This Rosicrucian tool helps us change a chaotic mind into a contemplative one. This is the only way we can see clearly and think rationally in our modern age. Meditation has been used for centuries to achieve the ultimate goal of mysticism, the union with God.

Grounding

Grounding is an important piece of the Rosicrucian tool kit. Grounding is a method of psychic protection. It comes into play when having to deal with a psychic attack, curses, black magic, and the like. Grounding protects our auric field by whipping up a protective layer covering our astral body. It is not a subtle tool, but it is an effective one. The practice of grounding can help you find your center in this world. On a physical level, when we are grounded, it means our feet are firmly planted on the ground. This is how it works on an astral level as well. When our feet are firmly planted, we are not swayed by the storms of life. Grounding helps us to develop the willpower necessary to succeed in this world. It can help you focus on your goals.

Grounding forces you to bring your mind back into the here and now. This is essential for survival in today's materialistic world. The practice of grounding helps us find our way in the world. It teaches us not to be dependent on anyone but ourselves. This can help us achieve great things in our lives. The idea of grounding is to walk barefoot outdoors and let the earth's energies flow through us, helping us relieve stress and recharge our batteries.

When your auric field is open, you are more receptive to energies of both the good and bad sort. Suppose you do not pay attention to your energy. In that case, you can become a channel for negative energies that bring misfortune into your life. Negative entities can use your auric field to access this world. They can even take control of your physical body and cause havoc here below. Grounding helps keep your auric field closed, protecting you from "bad vibes."

Shields

When the dangers of life threaten us, shields are put up to protect ourselves. They can become an impenetrable wall, blocking any negative energy whatsoever. Shields are a constant psychic barrier that remains in place around you at all times. They can be seen as an invisible energy field that keeps us safe from harm.

Grounding and shielding go hand in hand, with grounding giving us the strength we need to empower our shields. This is why we need both grounding and shielding for maximum protection! A shield is a wall that wards off negative energies. It can bounce back any negative energy directed at you before it reaches its target. This is a skill that needs practice to be mastered. Some psychic attacks are very strong and take a lot of strength to ward off. Negative entities cannot break through well-developed shields.

Shields can be as strong as diamonds, keeping away bad vibes of any sort. They shield us from the psychic vampires out there who want to suck our energy and make us weak. They block out any psychic attack and the like, keeping our auric field closed to negative energies. Our shields do not allow any negative energies to penetrate them. They can be a psychic shield that works like a mirror, reflecting any negative energy back to its sender.

Shields can be a wall that keeps us safe from the danger of the outside world. They are not barriers but rather metaphysical walls that keep negativity from getting to us. The strength of your shield depends on how much psychic energy you put into its construction. Shields come in different colors and shapes, depending on the nature of the energy you want to shield. As you develop your psychic abilities, you can fine-tune your shields and make them even more effective. Like anything else in esoteric practice, shields take practice and patience to master.

Daily Practice for Protection

The best insurance against black magic is to practice grounding and shielding daily. Visualize your protective white light surrounding you like a cloak at all times. The more often you practice this, the better you will become. You can also surround yourself with divine white fire whenever you require protection if you don't feel comfortable working with your energy.

You can also call on Archangel Michael for protection. He is the one we go to when we need protection of any sort, and he is the leader of the angels. He is responsible for keeping order in heaven and preventing any catastrophes from happening here below. The archangels are the ones who are responsible for protecting our planet from negative energies.

The daily practice of being grounded will keep your shield in place. No matter what job or task you are doing, when you ground, always remember to do the grounding exercise before going about your business. You never know when negative energy might try to get inside your auric field and cause some mischief.

Prayers and Mantras

Prayer is one of the best ways to keep your shield in place. Prayer can help create a spiritual connection between you and God. As you pray, visualize your shield around you. Praying helps to strengthen the connection between you and your higher self. It also strengthens your connection with the angels.

Prayer works best when you take a few minutes every morning to sit quietly and recite it out loud. You can pray for protection or use any prayer you like, and Mantras are also good for keeping your shield in place. As always, be careful not to overdo it, as anything that is done excessively can be harmful.

Anyone who practices magic should reflect on what he is doing before he does it and always keep safety in mind. Taking the time to think about what you are doing will help to keep you safe from any accidents that might arise if your mind wanders off elsewhere. Don't neglect visualization when working with any magickal tools. Visualization is very important when dealing with energy, and it helps to keep everything in your auric field under control. The more you practice this, the better you will become.

Night-Time Visualization

The act of visualization is very important for keeping your auric field safe and sound. If you visualize your energy following the proper path inward and outward, you will have much more control over it. The moment you visualize your energy moving in this fashion, negative energies are unable to penetrate your auric field.

The only people capable of breaking through your auric field are those who can see it. However, those who can see auras will not be able to read your thoughts. The only way they will be able to see your aura is if you are projecting it. If you are grounded and aware of your auric field, you are in total control of it at all times.

To practice this nightly visualization, sit down and relax. Close your eyes and take several deep breaths before beginning the exercise. When you are ready, visualize the events of your day, starting with the events of the evening and working backward to all the events that transpired in the morning. This technique is especially effective for those who have a difficult time recalling things from the past. In addition to keeping you grounded, this nightly exercise will also help you to stay on track throughout the day.

Do this magical exercise for a month, and your shield will be in place. You will then be ready to work with any sort of magick that you want to work with, including your daily meditation. Keep in mind that anything done excessively can be harmful, so don't forget to give your auric field a break every once in a while. This exercise helps to put you back into harmony with yourself. It also teaches you how to control your thoughts and actions.

All of these exercises will help you to stay in tune with who you are throughout the day and will give you more insight into the Law of Cause and Effect.

The Law of Cause and Effect

It is a good idea to be aware of the Law of Cause and Effect when working with any magickal tools. Any spells or rituals that are performed will come back to you three-fold. This means that any spell you cast will come back to you three times stronger than it was when you sent it out. If, for some reason, you do not want the outcome of a spell to occur, do not cast the spell in the first place. The same goes for everything else we do throughout our day, including our thoughts and actions. Everything we do will come back to us three-fold, so we must be mindful o before we act or speak. Your actions can affect the way people view you and view your message.

There are plenty of tools that you can use in your quest for spiritual growth. There is no need to stick with one tool or another, but you must be aware of the implications of everything you do. It's important to take some time out daily to practice grounding and visualization. If you experience any problems, contact a local metaphysical store for assistance, or do your research online. The tools listed in this chapter are all safe to use and will benefit you in one way or another. It is up to you to choose the path that best suits your needs and will allow you to grow spiritually.

Bonus I: The Secret Signs of the Rosicrucians

The Secret Signs of the Rosicrucians originated with a medical doctor and occultist, Franz Hartmann, who drew upon The Universal White Brotherhood, a loosely organized occult society with branches in Europe, America, Asia, and Australia, for their teachings. Hartmann incorporated the sixteen Secret Signs of the Rosicrucians in his book, The Life Beyond Death, first published in 1896. His writings brought the Secret Signs to light for the first time; previously, they were only passed down orally from member to member in the Universal White Brotherhood. This chapter will discuss each of the Secret Signs.

The Sixteen Secret Signs of the Rosicrucians

1. The Sign of Patience

This sign indicates that the adept is ready to wait for eons for the Divine Plan to unfold. And they are willing to be patient with themselves, others, and the process of life. The Sign of Patience is a call for peace, acceptance, and objectivity. It is used in the presence of someone who may be overly emotional to remind them to exercise patience and tolerance. By using this sign, the adept shows that they are serenely detached from the outcome.

2. The Sign of Kindness or Charity

The Sign of Kindness or Charity is an appeal for peace. This sign calls on the adepts to show kindness, sympathy, empathy, and benevolence to others. It also relates to the Rosicrucian doctrine that we should be gentle with ourselves and develop patience with our shortcomings. When the Sign of Kindness or Charity is used in public, it emphasizes that we should be compassionate and gentle, even with those who are hostile to us.

3. The Sign of Envying

The Sign of Envying is used when the Rosicrucian adept wishes to discourage envy or to call for gratitude. It appeals for self-awareness, self-regulation, and release from the emotional vulnerability associated with envy. This sign helps cultivate gratitude in the adept's life while discouraging feelings of discontent caused by coveting what others have. The Rosicrucian adept uses this sign when they are tempted to become envious.

4. The Sign of Lying

By using the Sign of Lying, the adept is calling for honesty and integrity in their lives. It is a reminder to be truthful with themselves and others. This sign can also come into play when someone feels they have been lied to or when they wish to lie in order to help themselves or someone else. The Sign of Lying can also be used when a group member feels the need to break a pact or promise.

5. The Sign of Covetousness

The Sign of Covetousness is an appeal for compassion and understanding. It is used to help the adept overcome their greed, materialism, and self-centered nature by encouraging contentment with what they have. By asking for a change of perspective, this sign develops your sense of compassion and awareness. It is used when you feel that you have been or are being deprived of something that you want.

6. The Sign of Wrath

When you feel enraged, this sign calls for self-control. It reminds you to refrain from violence and instead cultivate peace within yourself. This sign can also be used in situations where anger or violence is directed at you. The Sign of Wrath helps develop patience and self-regulation in your life and encourages nonviolence as a way of life.

7. The Sign of Boastfulness

By using the Sign of Boastfulness, you call on your higher mind to help you to overcome your pride and boastfulness. It is an appeal for humility, and it helps you to be grateful for your talents and abilities without needing to boast or brag. The Sign of Boastfulness reminds you about being humble, even when you have done or experienced great things.

8. The Sign of Arrogance

The Sign of Arrogance is used to help you to overcome your sense of superiority and call on the higher mind to be humbler. It calls for self-awareness, self-honesty, and self-regulation. The Rosicrucian adept uses this sign when they feel that they are better, smarter, or more capable than other people.

9. The Sign of Ambition

This sign is used to represent the Rosicrucian doctrine that we should aim high but not allow ourselves to be consumed by our ambitions. It encourages us to set our goals high but work with diligence and perseverance to achieve them. It also promotes self-discipline and is used when you feel overwhelmed by your ambition. The Rosicrucian adept uses this sign when they feel the need to lower their expectations or work more patiently and carefully toward achieving their goals.

10. The Sign of Justice

The Rosicrucian doctrine of Justice is a reminder to be fair and impartial to all people, even when we feel wronged or hurt by them. It is used to call on the higher mind for assistance with balance, self-control, or detachment. This sign teaches us that by being fair and just, we will be able to rise above our grievances. It is used when the adept feels that they are being treated unfairly or when they feel offended by something another person has said or done.

11. The Sign of Purity

The Rosicrucian doctrine of Purity reminds the adept at exercising moderation in all things, including speech, food, sexual expression, pleasure, and entertainment. It is used to develop control over the senses and help the user to avoid debauchery, addiction, or gluttony. This sign is also used to help you overcome your sense of guilt or shame. The sign encourages you to accept yourself as you are, without needing to feel guilty for past mistakes and experiences.

12. The Sign of Faith

This sign is used in the presence of someone who may not appear religious or spiritual to convey that they are part of the spiritual hierarchy. It is used to awaken faith, hope, and trust in others. The Sign of Faith also symbolizes that God's wisdom can be accessed at any time and that the guidance of the spirit guides is always available. This sign is a reminder to open up one's mind and heart and not let fear or doubt interfere with the process of listening.

13. The Sign of Love

This sign is used to convey an atmosphere of love and harmony. It can also be used to help others feel more peaceful and relaxed or to help them remember that we are all members of the human race. This sign can be used when we feel angry with someone to help the other person understand that we are not trying to hurt them but simply want them to feel more love. The sign calls on the higher mind to help us overcome our anger and sense of dislike toward them.

14. The Sign of Union

The sign of Union is used as a reminder that we are all one and that the Universe is an expression of singular unity. It also represents God's promise to bring us together in a deeper understanding of the truth. This sign is used to help dissolve conflicts and promote harmony, especially when it is difficult to unite our feelings with someone else's. It calls on the higher mind to help us find this greater truth and unify our experiences with another person in love and understanding.

15. The Sign of Labor

The sign of Labor represents the Rosicrucian teaching that we should work diligently to achieve our goals. It also represents the principle of Karma and reminds us that we must be careful with what we create, as it will return to us. This sign is used to help focus the energy of our thoughts, words, and actions. It helps us remain humble through our hard work. The sign reminds us that every idea, thought, and word carried out in action is magnified tenfold. It also reminds us to always be grateful for the gifts that we have been given.

16. The Sign of Self-Sacrifice

People use this sign to remind themselves that they need to be willing to give up their attachments in order for spiritual growth to occur. This sign is used to call on the higher self for discernment while discarding what is not of value and developing a deeper connection with the spiritual self. When used in conjunction with the signs of Union, it helps us to understand that by giving of ourselves, we have more to share with others.

The sixteen secret signs that medical doctor and occultist Franz Hartmann created for the Fraternity of the Rosy Cross encourage us to live a life full of love, faith, hope, and understanding. The signs remind us that there are indeed spiritual guides who are always available to help us. They also encourage us to give of ourselves to gain the greatest rewards, including spiritual enlightenment and higher understanding. By practicing the secret signs of the Rosicrucians, we can better ourselves and help others.

Bonus II: Becoming Rosicrucian

To become a Rosicrucian, you must first be a truly honest seeker of knowledge and wisdom. You must have developed a discerning mind that does not stray to the left or right but seeks truth for its own sake. You must be willing to go wherever the search may take you and have a willingness to sacrifice preconceived notions or personal desires for truth. You must also be willing to put in the work necessary to make yourself worthy of the Order.

As students study various aspects of Nature, particularly that which has gone unnoticed or unexplored by modern science, they will begin to realize that there are many secrets yet to be revealed. There are forces at work in the world around us, sometimes visible and sometimes not that work in ways that are not always obvious. Those with open minds and hearts will realize there is more to the world than meets the eye, and those who cannot recognize this must either be blind, deaf, and dumb or else willfully ignorant.

Many paths lead to the Temple of Wisdom, but there is only one Temple. The wise student will not allow themselves to be distracted by schools or organizations that appear to offer more than they can deliver. They will keep their eyes on the goal and follow those signs which show them the way. This chapter has been written to provide a brief introduction for those who might wish to pursue further studies.

The Steps to Initiation

There are five steps to becoming a Rosicrucian that must be pursued in order. These are the Probationer, Neophyte, Zelator, Theoricus, and Practicus. There is an optional sixth step called the Portal. In all regular Masonic and Rosicrucian organizations, a period of probation precedes all higher degrees. The goal is the same for both, and this is to determine if the candidate has the necessary qualities to be admitted to the group.

The Probationer Degree

Every regular Masonic and Rosicrucian order is made up of three degrees, sometimes called the Blue Lodge, because, in olden times, the room where such meetings were held was decorated with blue cloth. The first degree is called the Entered Apprentice, or more commonly, just the First Degree. The second degree adds a few lessons to the first, and it is called the Fellow Craft Degree. The third degree, which is sometimes referred to as *Master Mason Degree*, adds still more lessons to those who have learned the knowledge of the first two degrees. While the first two degrees generally only require some memorization and theatrical presentations, the third degree usually requires some physical work such as climbing ladders or crawling through small spaces.

The Zelator Degree

The second degree is called the Zelator Degree. In certain organizations, this is often referred to as the "Introduction to Alchemy" or some similar title. Besides having more lessons and symbolic plays than the first degree, there is a requirement to memorize the elemental table of the Middle Pillar along with certain signs, grips, passwords, and other information. While the first degree is fairly simple to obtain, the knowledge of how to pass the tests for the second degree is generally reserved for those who have proven themselves.

The Neophyte Degree

As the candidate passes through the testing period, they are often given some basic knowledge to prepare them for the next degree. This is called the Neophyte Degree, or sometimes just "the Initiation," and it requires only a few weeks or months of study. It generally rests on one's understanding of Sun worship, alchemy, numerology, astrology, and other similar subjects.

A common tradition in Masonic groups is for the new candidate to choose a name by which they will be known in this degree. Often, they select their own in some way that reveals something about their personality and background. In this way, they announce their intentions as clearly as possible and show that they have at least some understanding of those arts which are so highly prized by Rosicrucians.

The Theoricus Degree

In most Masonic and Rosicrucian organizations, the next step is called the Theoricus Degree. It will give a person a deeper insight into metaphysics and alchemy as well as help build their character so they can learn to distinguish between right and wrong. The equivalent degree in Freemasonry is called the "Fellow Craft" or Second Degree. In Rosicrucian orders, it is usually called the "Practicus" Degree. This degree often includes lectures on such topics as the seven principles of alchemy and how they relate to one's psychic development, the uses of Sun worship, and what qualities a Rosicrucian should strive for in their daily lives.

The Practicus or Portal Degree

The final step to becoming a Rosicrucian is called the Portal Degree, or in Freemasonry, it is often referred to as the "Master Mason" degree. It adds more knowledge about astrology, alchemy, and other metaphysical ideas that help learn how to improve one's mental abilities. This stage of instruction brings together all that the candidate has learned up to this point, and they are given tools that will help them accomplish their ultimate goal of bringing order out of chaos. This degree often includes a series of lectures on the subjects of medicine, theosophy, and related disciplines.

The Preparation

In addition to the degree ceremonies, there are other requirements for becoming a Rosicrucian. It is very common for members of the Order to have an interest in many different areas of study. This allows them to gain a well-rounded perspective on the world and also helps them become familiar with a wider range of topics. In Rosicrucian Orders, it is often expected that the new member has a good understanding of these topics before they are allowed to join:

- **Astrology:** They should be familiar with the position of the Sun, Moon, and planets in the zodiac at the time of their birth.

- **Alchemy:** They should display an understanding of what alchemy is and how it relates to the Three Great Principles of Hermes Trismegistus. In addition, they should be able to do basic alchemical experiments and understand some of the basic symbolism found in alchemical imagery.

- **Magic:** The new member should have a general idea of what magic is and how it relates to other metaphysical ideas. If they are unsure, the Order may allow them to study relevant topics for a few months before they are accepted as a member.

- **Religious Studies:** They should be familiar with the basic stories and principles of several different religions. If they are still unsure, Rosicrucian groups may allow them to study Christianity and a few other religions for a short time before they are initiated.

Official Groups

Many different Rosicrucian groups have chapters in various parts of the world. Some of them are small, while others have many different chapters. These groups often have websites that are listed on the Rosicrucian Order website. These groups are all under the auspices of one of the many different recognized orders within Rosicrucianism. Some of the most well-known Rosicrucian Orders include:

- The Ancient and Mystical Order Rosae Crucis, or AMORC
- Societas Rosicruciana in America
- The Martinist Order
- Fraternitas Rosae Crucis, or FRC
- The Hermetic Order of the Golden Dawn
- The Builders of the Adytum, or BOTA

Resources

If you are interested in joining a Rosicrucian order, there are several good resources that you can use to find out more information about them.

- The Rosicrucian FAQ provides detailed information about how to join most Rosicrucian groups.
- The Official website of the Rosicrucian Order provides information about how to join AMORC.
- The Societas Rosicruciana in America website has information about how to join their group.
- The Martinist Order website has information about how to join their group, including a form that can be downloaded and sent in to begin the membership process.
- The FRC website has lots of information about joining their group.

- The official BOTA website has more information about how to join their group.
- The AMORC website has more information about Rosicrucianism in general, including articles about their history and beliefs.

Once the candidate has met all of these requirements, they are allowed to petition for membership in one of the Rosicrucian Orders. Some groups may allow them to take a brief test before they are allowed to enter the Order. After passing all of these requirements, they are accepted as new members and invited to participate in the ceremonies that will allow them to progress from one degree to another. At this point, they are told what steps must be taken before they will be allowed to progress on to the next degree.

Conclusion

What we've learned in this section is that we can see the originators and founders of the Rosicrucian Order were all Kabbalistic Hermetists, and thus they brought with them a significant influence from Alchemy and Merkavah Mysticism. The Rosicrucian Order is an astral magic order posited on mystical Judaism and Christianity. Several of the founders were Jewish Kabbalists, while several others were Christian mystics. All of these came together to create a mélange that makes up modern Rosicrucianism (and Freemasonry).

While it is true that there are some differences between the Kabbalah and the Merkavah, if you look at it closely enough, they can appear to be the same. This is mainly because Kabbalah has its roots in Merkavah, and the way that the doctrines of the Kabbalah were set down was through a book called Sefer Yetzirah – which is a guide to meditating on mystical Jewish Mysticism. The concepts of the spiritual underworld and Chakra systems are also very similar in both Kabbalah, Alchemy, and Merkavah. The Astral Body, the Seat of the Soul, and the Plane of Yetzirah are all part of this mystical system.

This guide has been created as a primer for those who would like to go further and delve deeper into the Rosicrucians and Esoteric Christianity teachings. We have tried to give you enough information so you can go off and find out more on this topic if you are interested. In the first chapter, we outlined Rosicrucianism properly for you and have given you some insight into the original

Rosicrucian Order. In the second chapter, we talked about who Christian Rosenkreuz was and the history of the Rosicrucian Order.

The third chapter covered the Mysteries of Hermes, and the fourth chapter went over Poimandres, a Gnostic text. The fifth chapter looked at the mystical system of Merkavah, including the various levels of heaven and their correspondences in the Kabbalistic Tree of Life. The sixth went over the Twenty-Two Paths of Enlightenment as well as the mystical journeys of the path and much more. The seventh chapter covered Alchemy and Kabbalah, looking at Yesod, Hod, and Netzach in the Kabbalistic tree of life. The eighth chapter is about practical Rosicrucianism and how to practice this system of mystical Judaism.

The ninth chapter covered the daily life of a Rosicrucian as well as many other important topics in great depth. In the Bonus chapters, we have given you some insight into the secret signs of the Rosicrucians as well as a quick guide to becoming a Rosicrucian. Finally, we have included a list of further reading for the serious student.

All of this has been a small glimpse into the complicated world of Rosicrucianism and Hermeticism. This guide has been created so that you can go out and further your knowledge in this field if you're so inclined. We have tried to give a solid foundation in Rosicrucianism and its related branches of Kabbalah, Alchemy, and Merkavah Mysticism. We hope that you found this guide to be educational, informative, and interesting as well as entertaining!

Part 2: Kabbalah and Tarot

The Ultimate Guide to Kabbalistic Tarot, Divination, and Astrology

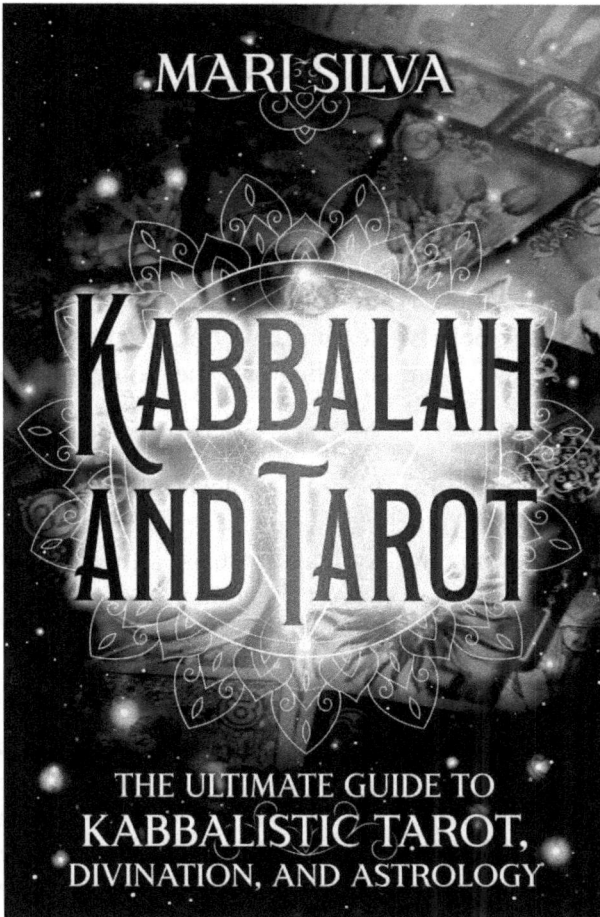

Introduction

This book is your ultimate guide to Kabbalah, Tarot, divination, astrology, and the links between these belief systems. It's intriguing yet still highly educational. You will learn how connections exist between the various elements of the Tarot and the worlds of the Kabbalah and how these connections act as a precursor or influence on a host of other beliefs. Reading this book, you will gain a deep and comprehensive understanding of the interpretation of the Tarot.

The book aims to give you the knowledge you need to use Kabbalah and Tarot together. It explores and explains various methods such as practical exercises, readings, astrological knowledge, divination, and Kabbalah rituals. We will introduce you to this mystical world if you are a beginner or attempt to enhance your knowledge if you are already a follower.

Unlike other books being sold on these topics, we not only present the parlor tricks that Tarot cards have to offer but also walk you through the deeper, more complex path of Kabbalah. Here, you will find a wide array of meditations and the history and interpretation of each of the Tarot cards. You will also come across impeccably detailed descriptions and associations of the different types of card decks.

It is the perfect source for beginners and experts alike. This book is an excellent addition to your library, whether you are unfamiliar with the Tarot, its symbols, and the tradition of

Kabbalah. The information given here is compressive for the more experienced readers looking to expand their knowledge.

This guide is also great for people who don't have any previous knowledge about either subject, as it offers an easy-to-understand exploration of how the Tarot and Kabbalah overlap and can work together.

The first chapter will walk you through an introduction to the rich history and origins of the Tarot and its popular symbols. Then, you will learn what the Tarot cards are as archetypal symbols and find out their connection with the Hebrew alphabet. Here, you will understand how each card leads to a path on the Kabbalistic Tree of Life. Chapter three covers the meaning of Jewish Mysticism and explains how Kabbalah is practiced. It also provides hands-on methods to perform various mystical practices, prayers, meditations, and rituals of Kabbalah.

Reading the following chapter, you will gain a deeper understanding of what the Tree of Life is. You will also learn how it can practically be used in tandem with the Tarot through the ten minor cards. The next chapter is dedicated to interpreting all the cards that make up the Major Arcana and providing interpretations and Kabbalistic links. As you continue to read, you will come across the interpretations of the cards of the Minor Arcana and their Kabbalistic correspondences. You will understand how these cards are more attuned to the physical world. The following chapter discusses the astrological and planetary inter-connections and other esoteric aspects through the lens of Kabbalah. Then, the book offers detailed instructions and imagery for spreads and how you can conduct a Tarot reading. The last chapter explores the other uses of Tarot cards besides readings. Here, you will learn all about the other divination and scrying methods that you can conduct using the cards. This chapter also explains how you can enhance your psychic abilities by using other tools, like crystals, alongside the Tarot cards.

Chapter 1: Wisdom of the Tarot Cards

With the centuries-old iconography that portrays a curious mix of religious allegories, ancient symbols, and several historic events, tarot cards have remained shrouded in layers of mystery. To critics and skeptics alike, the occult practice of reading the cards may seem to be irrelevant in modern-day life, but when you examine the tiny masterpieces, it is quite evident that they hold a lot of meaning, illuminating our complex desires and dilemmas. It does not take a clairvoyant to assess the popularity of tarot cards because, without a doubt, these illustrated cards have captivated the imagination of generations through the centuries.

An Overview of Tarot Card Etymology

Perusing the history of the Tarot, it is quite interesting that there were many names associated with them, including trionfi, tarocchi, or tarock. The word Tarot and the German word "Tarock" are derivations of the Italian "Tarocchi." The origin of the word "Tarocchi" is uncertain. However, the word "taroch" was used as a synonym for "foolishness" during the late 15th and early 16th centuries.

During the 15th century, tarot decks were exclusively called "Trionfi." This new name initially appeared around 1502, in Brescia, as Tarocho. Later, in the 16th century, another game gained popularity that used a standard deck but shared a similar name (Trinofa). The advent of this new game coincided with the former being renamed "tarocchi." According to modern Italian, the term Tarocco (a singular), as a noun, means a cultivar of blood orange. "Tarocco" is a verb attributed as referring to something that is either forged or fake. This interpretation is directly linked to the renaissance game of tarocchi as played in Italy, where a tarocco indicated one card that another could replace.

Tarot is basically a pack of cards that dates back to the mid-14th or 15th century and was popularly used in several regions of Europe (for instance, the Italian tarocchini, Austrian Konigrufen, and French tarot). But what's more intriguing is that the art of reading Tarot cards remains a part of our society even today.

A Peek through the History of Tarot

Tarot cards originated in Italy during the 1430s, and the game, as it was then, was played simply by adding a fifth suit of 21 uniquely illustrated cards to the four-suited regular pack. These illustrated cards were called trionfi or triumphs, which became the equivalent of a trump card. There was another card known as the fool or "matto." Although it sounds similar, it must not be confused with the modern-day "joker" card, which was invented during the 19th century and used during the euchre game as an unsuited jack. Interestingly, tarot cards crossed about nine levels and reached the status and state they are in today.

An interesting thing to note is that the overall meaning of divination cards has changed over time. This was greatly influenced by the culture of each era and the specific needs of people during that particular time.

The 15th Century Italian Cards

During the 15th century, in the Court of Ferrara, Milan, and Florence, Tarot cards gained rapid popularity. They started as the game of Tarocchi, which was quite similar to the game of bridge. The card deck consisted of four Minor Arcana suits (Swords, Coins, Batons, and Cups). However, several artists began adding trump cards to the deck with time, and this trend gradually created the Major Arcana. Generally, the trump card motifs were very different from the others and portrayed popular classical themes of the era. Many tarot decks were extremely expensive because they were customized and hand-painted with detailed dedication. This also meant that a set of tarot cards was initially only available to the elite as their price was high and out of reach for the average person.

Some of the earliest instances of tarot card rules can be found in a manuscript from the 15th century, written by Martiano da Tortona (the secretary to Milanese Duke Filippo Maria Visconti and who was a chancellor at the time). This compilation described a tarot card deck as having a total of 60 cards, including 44 cards with images of different birds (turtle dove, eagle, phoenix, and dove), another 16 cards decorated with Roman gods portraits (Mercury, Jupiter, Apollo, Ceres, Bacchus, and Cupid). According to Tortona, all the gods ranked above the order of birds and ranks of the images portrayed in the card deck. So, according to this, the 16 god cards were the trump cards.

Tarot Cards and the Catholic Controversy

This dates back to 1423, a time marked by fires in Bologna. Followers of Bernadino of Sienna, a Franciscan missionary and Italian priest, threw all the playing cards into the fires. Bernadino of Sienna was a strong systematizer and advocate of Scholastic economics. He preached against gambling, sorcery, infanticide, homosexuality, usury, Jews, and witchcraft – and was quite popular. Ironically, there is no hard evidence that tarot cards were also burnt, but these acts of burning playing cards emerged due to the belief that these represented anti-religious activities.

During the late 15th century, the Catholic Church put a strict ban on gambling but aristocratic games, including tarot cards, were exempt from these regulations simply because the Church wanted to keep the ruling class involved in religious activities. Shortly after the Reformation, the Church strongly objected to a set of cards that depicted a Papess and Pope. The card-makers started to paint less controversial figures on the cards to resolve this problem. You will see these images on the cards today as the High Priestess and Hierophant.

Gradually but steadily, the popularity of tarot cards as a game of choice spread across Europe because of their increased accessibility through a price drop after the printing press was invented.

Taking the French Route

During the 1490s, the French successfully conquered some parts of Italy and Milan, and many tarot card manufacturers moved to France. During the start of the 16th century, the Tarocchi cards became extremely popular in France and took the name "Tarot Cards." The deck that was becoming popular in France was quite similar to the version used in Milan, but in France, the deck further evolved and became known as "Tarot de Marcille," which is the standardized structure of a vast majority of tarot card decks used today.

The 18th Century Etteilla

In the 18th century, people started using tarot cards for divination through cartomancy and tarot card reading. This trend of using the tarot cards for divination led to a new wave of custom decks specially designed for occult purposes.

The 18th century was a time of immense political upheaval for the French because the ideals of the American War of Independence were fueling the French Revolution. France was effectively purged of its royal hierarchical system for quite some time. Mystical and occult-related things gained immense popularity during that era because they assured eternal life and quick wealth.

In Paris, during the 1770s, Etteilla, a French occultist, wrote a book on cartomancy and talked about using Tarot cards for fortune-telling. Quite interestingly, this was the very first historical record of Tarot cards being used for fortune-telling or the purpose of divination.

He published another book, entitled "How to Entertain Oneself with the Deck of Cards called Tarot," This book served as the first manual for reading Tarot cards for fortune-telling. It also included information about the possible origin of the Tarot deck and dated its origin from ancient Egypt. Etteilla published the first customized Tarot card deck for the sole purpose of fortune-telling or divination during 1789. He also started a school of Tarot and Astrology, and one of his students, D'Oducet, wrote a book that followed where Etteilla's left off and explained the meaning of Tarot cards in the light of Etteilla's teachings. This book laid down the foundation for several meanings and interpretations of the Minor Arcana in Rider-Smith's deck.

The Egyptian, Hebrew Connections, and Kabbalah

In 1781, Antoine Court de Gebelin wrote the very first essay linking the Tarot to ancient Egypt and the Hebrew alphabet in "Le Monde Primitif." Antoine Court de Gebelin was a former Protestant minister and a French Freemason whose complex analysis of the possible origin of Tarot cards led to the discovery that the cards could be somehow linked to the esoteric secrets of the Egyptian priests.

In 1856, Eliphas Levi published a treatise titled "Dogma and Ritual of Transcendental Magic," which proved to be an astoundingly influential document during the western occultist wave. This was the first-ever work that linked Tarot and Kabbalah. In this body of work, Eliphas linked the Hebrew alphabets with each Tarot card and then placed the cards on the tree of life. Eliphas Levi Zahed was a poet, French esotericist, and author who published twenty books about Kabbalah, alchemical studies, magic, and occultism. It is interesting to note that initially, Eliphas was an active member of the Catholic Church and pursued an ecclesiastical career. However, after some personal challenges, he left the Roman Catholic priesthood. He started disseminating knowledge of the occult around the age of 40 and swiftly gained a reputation as a ceremonial magician.

Levi's works inspired and attracted many acolytes in London and Paris, and his followers included artists, symbolists, romantics, and esotericists. Soon after that, Falconnier Wegner cards were created in 1896, and these were the first genuinely Egyptian card decks based on the descriptions of Paul Christian (Levi's follower).

The Golden Dawn of Tarot Cards

Toward the end of the 19th century, the stranglehold of the Church was finally fading away, and in 1888 Samuel Liddell Mathers and William Westcott (who were the renowned members of the fraternal organization known as "Freemasons") started the "Hermetic Order of the Golden Dawn in London." This "order" was created to function as a secret society that was dedicated to practicing and studying metaphysics, occult, and paranormal activities. So, during the 19th or 20th century, such records are quite easily found.

In contrast, the English-speaking world was largely unaware of tarot cards, except for some scholars who spoke French and were able to read the works of Eliphi Levi. The English scholar Kenneth Mackenzie revised Levi's writings and was popular throughout the Golden Dawn era. W.B. Yeats was also attracted to this group, and it became the very first Masonic order to welcome women. It also served as a nurturing ground for some highly influential personalities, including A.E. Waite and Aleister Crowley.

The American Tarot Cards

Populism and capitalism also contributed to the popularity of Tarot cards in America, doing so in a manner vastly different from what had happened in Europe. It was not merely because of the magic associated with Tarot cards but the complex literature, costs, and secret societies that set Tarot cards firmly out of reach to many people. Coincidentally, in America, the Tarot cards which were the most popular were the pirated Waite-Smith decks. Sales of these decks were often made after public lectures and lessons.

At the beginning of their arrival in America, the Tarot cards were completely disconnected from their Italian roots and had a mysterious air of esotericism around them. By the year 1915, several major European decks made their way to America. During this era of the Golden Dawn, many temples were established in New York and other cities. Another important historical event was when Paul Foster Case left New York in 1920 and invested his time and energy into making the Tarot card decks more affordable and accessible to the general public. He started by organizing public lectures, issuing pamphlets, and writing various articles on the matter. Later in 1937, Israel Regardie, who happened to be Aleister Crowley's former secretary, immigrated to America and re-issued Golden Dawn's previous secret teachings about the Tarot card decks.

The Modern Age for Tarot Cards

During the 1960s, Eden Gray, a writer exploring esoteric aspects of tarot cards and an American actress, wrote her very first book "Tarot Revealed: A Modern Guide to Reading the Tarot Cards." This book laid out simplistic guidelines that were quite easy to follow, and this brought a certain degree of user-friendliness to users of Tarot cards, thereby making tarot card reading more accessible to the public. According to Eden Gray, anyone can read Tarot cards easily. It has more to do with being intuitive while doing the readings rather than memorizing the whole deck. This belief is quite popular even today.

Because of efforts to demystify Tarot cards, many people started practicing the art of playing tarot. Another innovative idea was that

Tarot cards could be read or interpreted in several ways. This belief inspired many people to create their own customized tarot decks and attach their subjective interpretations to the symbols and archetypes. In short, reading Tarot cards has become a form of art.

Tarot cards have been adapted to our fast-paced, modern-day society and the associated lifestyle changes to blend in. Women-oriented decks with Goddesses, decks including people of color, or other special decks have been popular since the '70s. Several decks portray different cultures and their associated symbols and archetypes. For example, the <u>Xultun Tarot</u>, published in 1976 by Peter Balin, was the first to use illustrations from a non-European culture.

The Classical Tarot Card Decks

Today's standard tarot deck is usually based on the Piedmontese or Venetian tarot, with 78 cards. These were then grouped into two categories; the Major and Minor Arcana. The Major Arcana has up to 22 cards, commonly known as "trumps," and the Minor Arcana has 56 cards in the deck. Although several tarot decks are in use today, three decks are considered classics nowadays; the Tarot of Marseilles, Visconti-Sforza, and Rider-Waite Tarot deck.

Tarot of Marseilles

This tarot card deck (known as Tarot of Marseilles or Tarot of Marseille or Tarot de Marseille) came as a standard pattern of Italian-styled cards and was popular during the 17th and 18th centuries in France. Initially, it was made in Milan. It then grew in popularity and was used in Northern Italy, France, and Switzerland.

Like many other tarot card decks, this deck has 56 cards in four standard suits (Batons, Epees or Swords, Coupes or Cups, and Deniers or Coins). These cards start from an Ace and count up to 10. There used to be a practice of ranking the cards in a pattern starting with the 10 going to the Ace in suits of coins and cups, in line with other such games better known outside Sicily and France. In addition to these cards, there are four face cards in each suit (Valet or Knave or Page, Chevalier or Cavalier or Horse rider or Knight, Dame or Queen, and Roi or King). In the terminology of occult practitioners, this set of cards is known as Minor Arcana (also known as Arcanes Mineures).

These cards were originally printed from woodcuts and then colored by hand later on. The pattern of this deck gave rise to several tarot packs later on. This pack was also the first one to be used in occult practices and fortune-telling.

Visconti-Sforza

The Visconti Sforza deck is a collection of about 15 decks from the mid-15th century. These are also among the oldest surviving tarot card decks and were commissioned by the Duke of Milan, Filippo Maria Visconti, and his son-in-law Francesco Sforza, who also had a significant role to play in card numbering, interpretation, and visual composition. As a result, this deck demonstrates a curious glimpse into the lifestyle of nobility during the Renaissance period in Milan.

One of the supposedly oldest tarot decks, the Visconti-Sforza tarot card deck, was originally manufactured to entertain the aristocracy during the 15th century. In later years, it gradually became linked with the power of fate, occult secrets, and divination. These cards were also hand-painted by several renowned artists of that era. The cards feature stunning, hauntingly beautiful, and authentic imagery from medieval times. This deck contains 22 allegorical and mystical trump cards as well.

There are three particularly renowned sets associated with this card deck, Pierpont Morgan Bergamo, that originally had 78 cards (15 face cards, 20 trumps, and 39 pip cards). The second set of cards is Cary Yale (also known as the Visconti di Modrone set) and dates back to 1466. This set contained 67 cards made up as follows (17 face cards, 11 trumps, and 39 pip cards). This card set is the only known classical western set that has six ranks of face cards. The third set is "Brea Brambilla," named after Giovanni Brambilla. This set contains 48 cards and has two trumps (wheel of fortune and the Emperor). All the pip cards have a silver background, while the face cards have a gilt background.

Rider-Waite Tarot Deck

This deck is another popular classical tarot card deck known as the Rider-Waite-Smith, Waite-Smith, or Rider tarot deck. The deck features simple images but detailed backgrounds, containing a lot of symbolism. According to many, this is considered to be the most amazing Tarot deck. Some Christian imagery was removed from this deck, and other symbols were added. For instance, the "Pope" card was replaced with "Hierophant," while the "Papess" card was replaced with "High Priestess." Also, the Lovers card that depicted a clothed couple receiving a blessing from a cleric or a noble (in a medieval scene) was replaced by naked imagery of Adam and Eve in the Garden of Eden, with the Ace of cups now featuring a dove with Sacramental bread. Suffice it to say, the imagery and symbols used in this deck were influenced by 19th-century occultist and magician Eliphas Levi and the Hermetic Order of the Golden Dawn.

The vibrant cards in this deck were published in 1909 by the Rider Company according to the instructions of mystic and academic A. E. Waite and have illustrations by Pamela Colman Smith. Dr. Arthur Edward Waite was a renowned scholar and preacher of occultism and published a book entitled "The Holy Kabbalah and The Key to the Tarot," first issued in 1910 in England. According to Waite, symbolism held the key to efficiently interpreting the Tarot pack. The deck features 78 cards, including 56 Minor Arcana, which fully depict the scenes with symbols and figures.

Chapter 2: The Tarot in Kabbalah

"Today, we see the Tarot as a kind of path, a way to personal growth by understanding ourselves and life."

— Rachel Pollack, Seventy -Eight Degrees of Wisdom

According to some traditions, the angel Metatron endowed humanity with the gift of Tarot and Hebrew letters, and these were preserved as a prized secret of mystical traditions that were kept out of reach from the public. Later on, due to theft, portions of these teachings were passed through Arabia, Egypt, and Europe, and it became popularly known as the Tarot card deck with obscure symbols and imagery. This deck has been re-arranged, degenerated, misused, and misinterpreted for centuries.

According to folklore, the angel gave Hebrew letters and tarot to mankind to help us see things clearly, beyond our limited and confused psychological state. Therefore, Tarot is a sacred and ancient method of gaining spiritual knowledge and insight, and Kabbalah is the science behind it. Kabbalah is about numbers that reveal the structures of our Universe and offers a way out from suffering.

The Tarot cards and Kabbalah, together, energize, clarify, and empower our spiritual lives, and instead of getting stuck in assumptions or guesses, one can be sure about something that is learned through Kabbalistic Tarot. However, it may still come as a surprise that Tarot card decks are strongly linked with Kabbalah, but to comprehend this connection better, you would have to understand what Kabbalah entails.

A Brief Overview of Kabbalah

Kabbalah (or Qabala), translated literally, means "correspondence" or "reception, tradition" and is an obscure method of discipline in Jewish mysticism (it's considered a school of thought). According to Judaism, a traditional Kabbalist was often called "Mekbul."

Interestingly, there are many definitions of the Kabbalah in place that are mainly dependent on the aims and traditions of the followers. The religious origin of Kabbalah entails it as an integral component of Judaism that was later adapted in the Western esotericism (Hermetic Qabalah and Christian Kabbalah).

The Jewish Kabbalah

Jewish Kabbalah involves certain esoteric practices and teachings explaining the relationship between the Eternal God, Ein Sof (the infinite), and the finite, mortal universe. In short, this forms the very foundations of mystic interpretations found within Judaism. According to the general Jewish tradition, Kabbalah, as a belief system, came from Eden as a revelation to guide the election of righteous people and was a privilege shared by few.

Christian Cabala

The Christian Kabbalah, commonly known as Cabala, dates back to the Renaissance era when Christian scholars started developing a strong interest in the mystic practices of Jewish

Kabbalah. However, these scholars attached their own Christian interpretations of the Kabbalah. This interest in the Cabala originated because of a strong desire to add more mystical meanings and interpretations to several aspects of Christianity.

Hermetic Qabalah

The third offshoot of Kabbalah was known as Hermetic Qabalah (meaning accounting or reception). This happens to be an esoteric Western tradition that involves occult and mysticism. This is the one that laid the framework and foundational philosophy for several magical and mystical-religious societies, including the Thelemic orders, Golden Dawn, Builders of Adytum, and Fellowship of the Rosy Cross. Hermetic Qabalah also served as a significant precursor to the Wiccan, New Age, and Neopagan movements. It is also the foundation of the Qliphothic Qabala (followed by Left-Hand Path orders, like the Typhonian Order). This also grew simultaneously with the Christian Cabalistic movement during the era of European Renaissance.

Interestingly, Hermetic Qabalah draws on several influences, including Western astrology, Pagan religions, Jewish Kabbalah, Alchemy, especially influences from Greco-Roman and Egyptian alchemy, Gnosticism, Neoplatonism, Enochian system of angelic magic of Edward Kelley and John Dee, tantra, hermeticism, and tarot symbolism. It is different from the Jewish Kabbalah by being a more widely assimilatory or syncretic system, but it does share several concepts with the Jewish Kabbalah.

How Are Kabbalah and Tarot Linked?

Many members of these societies are still unaware that Kabbalah and Tarot are strongly interconnected. Kabbalah has an important role to play in tarot cards. There are several mysterious origins linked with Tarot cards. For instance, some are linked to 13th century France (as depicted in the Marseilles deck), while others date back to ancient Egypt, and still others that proclaim their origins hail from Italy. But the question that causes curiosity to many is how the art of Tarot relates to Kabbalah or Jewish mysticism.

Looking back to 1856, it is quite clear that all of this started around the time when Eliphas Levi was successful in publishing his very first book. Levi talked in detail about the Major Arcana and how it is related to the Hebrew alphabet. It was quite interesting to go through Levi's text because of the keen observation and comparisons that he drew. Levi's book also elaborates on the suits of Minor Arcana and interestingly highlights an overlap or a relationship with the name of the God (sometimes referred to as "Tetragrammaton")! However, after Levi's book, his student, Papus, also followed in the footsteps of the teacher and came up with a similar book on Tarot. Papus's book was titled "The Tarot of Bohemians," and it was an interesting record. While all of this was happening, Oswald Wirth was working on creating a whole new deck of the Major Arcana with Hebrew designs and letters.

What is more interesting is that several renowned Tarot experts were in favor of these changes and perspectives, including Aleister Crowly. One such example is when Crowley actually altered the Emperor and Star and swapped them with Hebrew letters. So, according to Crowley's version, the "star" represented "heh" while the "Emperor" represented "tzaddi."

To quote the exact words of Crowley, from his famous book, titled "The Book of the Law," in chapter 1 of the book, he writes... "All these old letters of my Book aright, but Tzaddi is not the Star."

If this were any less interesting, it would be worth mentioning here about the Rider-Waiter and Golden dawn decks because they also incorporated Hebrew. Although you would not find the Hebrew letters appearing on these cards, Waite mentions this relationship in his writings.

To put everything in simple words, the four different suits of the Tarot deck would relate to many facets of our life and the diversity of our humane journey through many seasons of this world. Wands represent passion, as well as sexuality, while swords were connected with knowledge, cups denoted emotions, and pentacles were for money or career.

This shows us that we can indeed receive guidance and fulfillment from the universe around us. As we mentioned at the beginning of the chapter, Kabbalah essentially means "receiving." This makes a lot of sense in that we are, in a way, receiving what we require from the universe around us, and we fail to comprehend it fully.

According to Judaism, God is unnameable, unknowable, and undefinable, which relates perfectly to our journey in Tarot. Here it would be much more interesting to share the exact words of Kliegman:

"The most important thing to know about Kabbalah is very simple: Kabbalah means "receiving." We are dealing with an explanation of the creation in terms of a generous God. (Kabbalistically, the godhead is twofold. There is Adonai, the male aspect of the godhead, the Lord. And there is the Holy Shechinah, the female aspect of the godhead. We are dealing with an androgynous spirit, not to be understood as male but as the divine ruling spirit, the Eternal One. Basic to the Kabbalistic system, then, is that the universe is created by a loving God whose wish is to give and who has created us specifically as creatures who can receive, with loving awareness and conscious appreciation. We have choices to make, and we can fall into evil ways, but we are born perfect."

David Krafchow's book on Kabbalistic Tarot, gained immense popularity among the interested factions, and rightly so because of the much relevant and historically significant content that he shared. If we peruse the book of David Krafchow, he talks at length about the intriguing history (linked with Jews) of the quests for the self and truth and about the Hebraic perspective regarding the Minor and Major Arcana. Therefore, the Tarot card decks are a tool to find the truth, and these cards are believed to hold their roots in the early Jewish mystic traditions. The configuration of symbols and images that are embedded in the cards reflects the ancient esoteric knowledge, referred to as "Cabala."

According to Dovid Krafchow, we have to explore the tarot's cabalistic elements and historical roots to get the truest and fullest meaning from this age-old instrument. For instance, you can see the High Priestess holding a Torah and sitting between the pillars of King Solomon, surrounded by pomegranates. This card is interesting because it represents a curious search for knowledge that is, indeed, confined because of humane limitations and experiences, and it poses an interesting irony. In addition to this, the card draws on the universe to offer guidance to the querent or seeker while searching for a way to balance the gender binaries.

To understand this better, let's go back to the time of the Greek invasion of Israel. During the time of the invasion of Israel by the Greeks, the Jews were forbidden by the Greeks to study Torah, so the Jewish believers invented a secret method to study the Torah that apparently looked like playing cards simply to pass their time. These were the very first tarot decks that initiated a study of the Torah in secrecy without being detected by their oppressors. As soon as the Maccabees expelled Greeks from Israel, the land once again resurfaced as the Kingdom of Jews, and tarot cards disappeared from sight. About 1500 years later, as a result of Jewish disputes with Catholic political and religious persecutions, Catholic theologians, and inquisition, the tarot cards came back.

Tarot and the Hebrew Alphabet

There are about four main views when it comes to correlating the tarot cards with Hebrew alphabets:

1. **Levi's View:** According to this, the Hebrew letters follow the order of the Major Arcana, sequentially except for the un-numbered Fool card, which is placed as a penultimate card.

2. **GD's View:** According to this view, the letters follow the Major Arcana order, and the Fool card has been numbered "zero," while Justice and Strength interchanged their numbering and position.

3. Crowley's View: According to the Hebraic letter allocations, that remains the same as the second view, except for the Star and Emperor cards; the rest of the cards reverse their GD letter allocations.

4. Filipa's' View: According to this view, the letters follow the order of the tarot cards (the Fool card remains unnumbered and placed as a 22nd card at the sequence end).

There is a great deal of overlap between the Torah and Tarot, from the Jewish imagery to the meaningful numbers. Before we move on, let's quickly refresh the anatomy of tarot, the basic deck has two parts: Major Arcana and Minor Arcana. The Minor Arcana has 56 cards, divided into four suits, with each suit having four face cards. The four suits are Wands, Swords, Cups, and Pentacles (or Coins) corresponding to Clubs, Spades, Hearts, and Diamonds. In comparison, the Major Arcana has 22 cards (there are also 22 letters in the Jewish alphabet) that are not divided into suits and represent karmic influence that is often thought of as life lessons.

In the book "Kabbalistic Tarot" Dovid Krafchow talks about how Tarot is the key to unlocking the essence of Kabbalah. Dovid drew similarities between the 22 Major Arcana cards and the Hebrew letters and four suits corresponding to four Kabbalistic worlds. Dovid also described the cards according to Kabbalistic interpretation and how it relates to the Torah and offered insights into the Tree of Life through various Kabbalistic readings. The four suits of the Minor arcana link to the four distinct journeys of our life. The "Swords" are about thought and knowledge, while the "Cups" are all about love and emotions, the "Pentacles" talk about wealth and health, and "Wands" have to do with passion, sexual energy, and creativity. The four Kabbalistic worlds of Yetzirah, Briah, Asiyah, and Atzilut are also associated with the four suits in the tarot deck that attach another dimension of meanings to the cards.

In addition to the obvious connection between the Hebraic alphabets and tarot cards, various other Jewish symbols are illustrated on these cards. You will understand this connection if you have seen the Rider-Waite deck (created in 1909). You can view the imagery on:

- **"Wheel of Fortune"** (this card is about the limitation of our free will and features a wheel with the word "TORA" written, as well as "יהוה" which is the unspoken Hebrew word for the God)
- **The Lovers'** (that is about being consumed by an idea and a person, and the card features the scene from Bereshit or Genesis from the Garden of Eden)
- **"The High Priestess"** (this card reminds us that we all have a certain sacred understanding within ourselves that has the answer to things for which we are searching. The card features a Priestess with a Torah in hand, sitting between the pillars of Solomon's temple).

Tarot and the Tree of Life

The "Tree of Life" can appear to be a complicated concept; however, one can understand it as an illustration of universal laws to shed light on the nature of reality. According to many interpretations of the Tree of Life, it is merely an eternal emanation of Divine principles (the concepts of macro and microcosm are quite relevant here) and is quite overlapping with the fractal. This tree of life is believed to be quite alive inside everyone – and each human being is seen as a branch of this tree. In other words, this tree represents a simple manifestation of matter in the form of energy and spirit. Traveling downward, we can find the subconscious and our body. When traveling towards the top in the Tree of Life, you will come across the source of soul (divinity) and our actualized or higher self. In essence, it's the richness of our inner life and a symbolic representation of the blueprint of creation.

The diagram has 22 paths, just like the 22 cards in the Major Arcana. These paths represent the lessons learned throughout life's journey or the spiritual needs that propel us to traverse to the next node (or level). These paths are also known as the Path of the Serpent and are about returning to the divine. Similarly, in tarot cards, the Major Arcana is about the Fool's journey, and the 22 paths in the Tree of Life offer yet another perspective. This interpretation is similar to Labyrinthos' philosophy and is about spiritual enlightenment in allegorical terms.

The Four Worlds and Tarot

Four Kabbalistic worlds correspond with a letter in God's name and represent a suit in the Minor Arcana in a deck of tarot cards. All four of these worlds relate to one another, and their nodes interlocked represent a link in the material and divine world. This structural representation is called "Jacob's Ladder" and is interpreted as a spiritual staircase leading straight to the heavens. Minor Arcana is a symbolic representation of these worlds (four in total), while the pentacles or element of earth is at the bottom of this staircase. The top of the staircase represents wands and fire.

The 10 Divine Powers or Sefirot

The ten nodes of the Tree of Life represent different aspects of the divine God, the psyche of the self. These are known as the Sefirot or Sephiroth or Sephirah in the Kabbalah. Since the top of the Tree of Life is the closest point to God and the bottom is closer to a manifestation of our material world, it is helpful to visualize the Sefirot as a bunch of mirrors reflecting the divine light from top to bottom. These numbered cards are related to Minor Arcana (world of emanation, as a beginning). The journey is towards the tens through the aces (the journey to the next world also starts with an Ace). For instance, we travel from the 10 of Wands to the ace of Chalices and from 10 of Chalices to the ace of Swords or 10 of Swords to the Ace of Disks. The 10 of Disks is the end because it is the home to matter, while the Ace of Wands is the closest point to the divine.

The Shekinah

The Shekinah (also known as Sacred Self) is considered the twin flame of the Holy Spirit and represents the feminine aspect of the Divine particle or God or the energy of creation. She exists as an "essence" instead of a being but also possesses the ability to manifest herself in different ways incomprehensible to mankind. She is also called the Sophia Christ in the Gnostic gospels and is acknowledged in Judaism. According to tradition, she is a powerful feminine voice and is there to bring balance and equality and to steer the world away from an all-masculine image of the Divine God. The actualization of a feminine divine through the symbolic illustrations of Shekinah is a significant achievement of Kabbalah.

In tarot, the concept of Shekinah is multifaceted and has many layers of complexity and meaningful interpretations to it. The Shekinah is sometimes considered to be the Moon and is attributed to the "Tau" letter, while in other instances, Shekinah is thought to be the firstborn Metatron. She is also believed to be living in the body or cosmos of kabbalists, which functions as the chariot of the Shekinah. Moreover, the Papess or High Priestess is often associated with the Shekinah, but that is only one interpretation.

The Pre-Kabbalistic Mekravah

Now that we have discussed various aspects that interlink Kabbalah with Tarot, another fascinating point is the Mekravah (also known as Merkabah or Merhavah), referred to as a chariot Mysticism and a famous school of early Jewish mysticism. The main Merkabah literature dates back to the 200-700 CE period, and the stories are about the ascension to the Throne of God and other heavenly palaces. Maaseh Merkabah (translated as "working of the chariot") was a new name for the Hekhalot text, which Gershom Scholem discovered. In the text, the concept of journeying to the heavenly divine hekhal is more of a spiritualization of the pilgrimages to the material (earthly) hekhal. It can be considered a form of pre-Kabbalistic Jewish mysticism, which is about the possibilities of journeying toward God and the ability of humans to draw the divine powers toward the earth.

The literature interlinking Tarot and Kabbalah is rich and has a mysterious occultist aspect. However, several important details are yet to be covered on this subject in the next chapters.

Chapter 3: Jewish Mysticism in Theory and Practice

As you have read in the previous chapter, Jewish mysticism (or Kabbalah) represents an extraordinary set of beliefs with traditions and teachings that differ radically from other mystic schools. Not only are Kabbalah and its conventional practices considered by its followers as an essential part of the Torah, but it also allows practitioners to partake in supernatural experiences. These journeys influence the lives of the mystics and enable them to change their course if they want to. The knowledge they seek stems from the premise that o the truth uncovers the secrets of life. A mystic's capacity to affirm the truth and live in it within their capacity is developed with rigorous practice – and it all begins with the Book of Creation.

Sefer Yetzirah

Part of a mystic's desire to establish a relationship with the creator is the need to understand the many layers of truth. Sefer Yetzirah (also known as the Book of Creation) is an ancient Jewish mystical work that describes how the universe was formed. You can also find directions for a meditative practice described in its short and somewhat mysterious passages; this may help you establish a connection with the creator. It's unclear when or where the book was written or if it had one or more authors. Sefer Yetzirah carved a path toward contemporary Jewish mystical tradition and practice through its unique way of structuring Kabbalistic wisdom. One of the main characteristics of the book is its relatability. Even those whose worldview and beliefs differ from the traditional Kabbalistic understanding can take advantage of its teachings.

According to Sefer Yetzirah, God created the universe by combining 32 different paths of wisdom. Twenty-two are letters of the Hebrew alphabet, present in the fabric of existence, while the other ten come from God's creative intentions. The latter is also known as *sefirot*, representing the physical dimensions of the universe. Since there are ten dimensions, there are also ten different frames within which the process of creation can unfold. Sefirot have two lists – one depicting the dimensional issue within the universe, the other dealing with the elemental substances.

Sefer Yetzirah's ability to lead its reader toward studying the physical universe is so practical. Unlike other teachings that focus on a hidden, mystical domain, this book displays and explains the multitude of realms in the cosmos available to explore. Mystics can interact with Sefer Yetzirah in two ways. You can either absorb the meaning of the individual letters one by one during meditation or use a similar thought-focusing exercise to explore the ten different dimensions by yourself.

Sefer Ha-Zohar

Sefer Ha-Zohar (or The Book of Radiance) is another well-known work of Kabbalistic literature, useful for scholars and mystics alike. According to Jewish mysticism, Sefer Ha-Zohar Zohar was revealed by God to the biblical Old Testament prophet, Moses, at Mt Sinai.

Initially, the content was passed from one generation to the next orally, until eventually, Rabbi Shimon bar Yohai wrote the teachings down around the second century. Its themes revolve around the creation of the universe and the nature of the creator itself. Like Sefer Yetzirah, it describes God's relationship to its creation through the sefirot and the revelation of the Torah. Numbers, letters, and words also represent the main building blocks. However, the teaching of Sefer Ha-Zohar also includes knowledge about evil, sin, exile, the commandments, the ancient Jewish temple, its priests, and the prayers they urge the followers to practice. The book provides mystics with the freedom to journey through history and their own imagination, where they can explore the mysteries of the Torah and much more. Essentially, its purpose lies in revealing the secret meaning of the Torah.

The ten sefirot are the expressions of God's nature, but they also serve as a template for our spiritual journey. In becoming a mystic, you can use them to establish a spiritual connection with God – the ultimate goal of the Kabbalah. Sefer Ha-Zohar suggests performing the spiritual contemplations during nighttime because this promotes the flow of creative processes. This allows you to observe processes in our world and the divine realm. Reciting prayers, meditating, or even studying mysticism during the night will take you much closer to God. In addition, the literary forms of Sefer Ha-Zohar probably represent the most extensive collections of Kabbalistic traditions. This gives those who seek spiritual enlightenment an unparalleled opportunity to study it extensively and develop their unique Kabbalistic practices. After all, the book itself depicts gaining knowledge as the highest form of connection to God.

Mystical Practices of Kabbalah

The Kabbalistic tradition is a rich source of Jewish mystical practices, rituals, and prayers. Most of them are related to finding a way to form a union with the creator, whereas a small percent of them are associated with the Tarot directly or indirectly.

Counting of the Omer

One of the most well-known ritual practices in Jewish mysticism is the "Counting of the Omer" (also known as "Sefirat ha Omer"). Its importance lies in its history and effortless performance, even for beginners. Essentially, the practice counts out the steps marking the 49-day journey of the Jewish people, starting from the second day of Passover, and ending the day before Shavuot. According to this religion, on the 50th day, God delivered the Law to Moses. For Christians, this event is widely known as Pentecost. The first 49 days are identified by their numbers, and a daily blessing is said each day.

This practice stems from a teaching of the Torah that people should mark the time between the barley harvest and the wheat harvest by offering sheaves of grain. The word omer can be translated to "sheaf," but it only refers to these offerings. In ancient times, people took a sheaf of barley as soon as they started to gather it and brought it to the temple to express their gratitude for the plentiful harvest. They continued to bring the sheaves until there wasn't any barley left to harvest. According to the Torah, it lasted 49 days (or seven complete weeks). On the 50th day, they were ordered to present a new meal offering to God – and this marked the day when they started to bring wheat.

Another meaningful interpretation of counting is related to the liberation of Jewish people from slavery in Egypt. Passover marks the date of the initiation of the liberation process, while Shavuot represents the culmination of the events. Counting up to Shavuot serves as a reminder of the time it took the Jewish people to awaken from a slave mentality and become an autonomous community.

Jewish rabbis preserved the obligation to count. Nowadays, people living in large communities start the process on the second night of Passover, while those in the diaspora integrate it into the second seder. The counting is considered valid only if it's done following its main principles:

- The counting is done each evening after sundown – as this is the time when the day begins according to the Jewish custom.

- No more than 24 hours should pass between two counting sessions- skipping a day in counting diminished the blessings for the rest of the days.

- The blessing should always precede the counting – so it's best to state the omer when one is finished with the rest of the ritual.

The good news is anyone can count the days, regardless of their experience with Jewish mysticism. If you happen to start your journey of exploring Kabbalah right around Passover, feel free to begin the practice. When initiating the count, you should begin with the following blessing:

"Barukh ata Adonai Eloheinu Melekh ha'Olam asher kid'shanu b'mitzvotav v'tizivanu al sefirat ha'omer."

In English: *"Blessed are you, Adonai our God, Sovereign of the Universe, who has sanctified us with your commandments and commanded us to count the omer."*

After reciting the blessing, you should state the appropriate day of the count, like this:

"Hayom yom echad la'omer"

In English: "Today is the first day of the omer."

When you reach the seventh day, you should also include the number of weeks you have counted on each following day. For example, if you are on the 13th day:

"Hayom sh'losha asar yom, she'hem shavuah echad v'shisha yamim la'omer."

In English: "Today is 13 days, which is one week and six days of the omer."

You can also start the entire process with a mediation that helps you focus on the intent of fulfilling the commandment of the Torah. Many mystics find this exercise useful in their devotions as it allows them to always keep their thoughts on the task at hand. It may also help if you try to identify each week with a different quality (human or divine) – and each day with a specific representation of those. This converts the practice into a spiritual journey, on which one can reflect on different moral issues after each week.

The Practice of the Kabbalistic Cross

As a fundamental routine in Kabbalah, the practice of the Kabbalistic Cross is a great way to draw spiritual power – whether you are at the beginning of your mystical journey or are well versed in this art. You use your body and mind to show devotion to the divine spirit and align yourself with its purpose. The exercise is also beneficial to strengthen your balance and composure, particularly if it's done daily for several weeks. You can even use it as a form of meditation to center your thoughts on one specific intent designed to help you reach your goals.

However, the practice of the Kabbalistic Cross is part of an extensive ritual. There are two different ways to perform the ritual Kabbalistic Cross. The first one is done at the initial stage of a ritual to invoke the divine spirit. The second one is performed after the ceremony and honors the divine power and blessings received during the ritual.

If you want to perform the Kabbalistic Cross on its own, it's recommended to opt for the first version. This one starts with you standing facing east, naturally relaxing your hands at your sides. Visualize the sky as a vast ocean called the Ain Soph Aur. It is filled with incandescent white lights and reaches beyond the horizon.

Deep breathing exercises will also help, as well as raising your hands above your head. Make sure your palms are pointed toward your head and the fingers are extended upwards, then recite the following:

"In your hands, oh ineffable one!"

Then, you should imagine the lights of the ocean forming a sphere above your head and slowly start lowering your hand toward your forehead. As you exhale, you should see the light descending as well, reaching your head just as you touch your forehead.

At this point, you say the word *"Is"* and focus on visualizing the beam of light moving down to the center of your body. With your right hand, you should follow its path until your fingers are pointing at your feet, where you should see a second beam of light forming at your ankles.

Now, you say the words *"The Kingdom"* while moving your right hand to your right shoulder, where you see the third sphere of light as you say, *"The Power."*

Then, you move your right hand toward your left shoulder, drawing light toward it, allowing it to travel through your body as you recite:

"And the Glory."

Now, place both of your hands on your heart, forming a cup with them, and speak:

"Forever and ever."

Lastly, you will focus your attention on the first globe of light still shining above your head and allow your arms to drop back to your sides while saying:

"Amen."

The second version isn't used outside of Kabbalistic rituals, although it isn't all that different from the first one. This starts by cupping your hands in front of your heart while visualizing a sphere of light in them. You raise your hands above your head toward the Ain Soph and say:

"Above my head shines your glory, oh ineffable one."

Lowering your left hand, you continue:

"And in your hands."

From this point, the ritual continues the same way as it does in the first version.

Since humans often find it impossible to conjure this image, you will need to practice it a few times. That said, even attempting to visualize the existence of this infinite realm is a beneficial spiritual exercise. Once you become comfortable with this exercise and have gained a measure of proficiency with the visualization aspect, you can proceed with learning more complex practices, such as the Middle Pillar Exercise.

The Middle Pillar Exercise

Designed to promote the balance of the body, mind, and soul, the Middle pillar exercise prepares followers for advanced spiritual practices. Typically, you would perform this exercise directly after completing the Kabbalistic Cross. You start by visualizing the remaining sphere of light penetrating the crown of your head. Then, you take a deep breath, followed by an extended exhale. During this exhale, focus on imagining the light from a column as it journeys through your body, descending toward your throat, where it forms another orb. From there, it travels into your chest, extending into yet another sphere around your heart.

You should take another deep breath and repeat the exhaling and visualizing part, seeing the process repeat again in the lower areas of your body until the column of light reaches your feet.

When you feel the light enveloping your ankles, redirect your focus to visualizing the sphere above your head. Focus on this light becoming brighter and brighter while holding your breath for a couple of seconds. This will allow you to feel the presence of the divine spirit and connect with it, even if you are a beginner.

When you are ready to move on to your next breath, you may turn your attention to the next orb around your throat. This is called Da'ath – and it helps you get in tune with the Divine and facilitates your connection with it. After a bit of practice, you will be able to see it turning into a gray light and flaring up in response whenever you are speaking to it. Moving on to the next source of light, the sphere of Tipareth, you can see it taking on a golden hue. The light at the lower part of the body is called Shaddai El Chai, and you should visualize it turning a deep purple color. Lastly, the orb at your feet should take on the colors of the sky or the earth, varying from turquoise to russet and even black. This one is the last light, centering upon the middle pillar – your body.

Once you visualize all the different lights, you should remain still for a few minutes. It's a good idea to hold this position for as long as you can concentrate on picturing the middle pillar. Try to hold the picture of all the spheres around your central column of light in your mind for as long as you can. This is particularly important for beginners, as it helps them further their visualization skills. It also allows you to become physically comfortable with this and similar demanding exercises. As a beginner, you should concentrate on holding the spheres in your mind, but soon, you will need to move on to connecting with them on a deeper level. Concentrating on their meaning, you develop a sense of how they are built and their purpose in this universe. After all, their reality is what holds the key to reaching the divine forces you seek in your practice – mystical or otherwise.

The Tradition of Tikkun Chatzot

Like many other Kabbalistic customs, the Tikkun Chatzot is also associated with the night's atmospheric ability to bring profound transformation into one's life. The ritual consists of prayers, Torah studies, and mediation from midnight to dawn. This practice dates back to the time of King David, when the importance of rising before sunrise had become predominant amongst Jewish mystics. It is believed that the dark hours amplify one's inner lights, pointing out whether someone needs to rectify something in their soul, make up for mistakes, or be shown the way toward divine consciousness. In addition, Jewish mystics believe that the predawn hours are the best time to deal with harsh spiritual forces and perform healing rituals.

The ritual starts with saying the introductory morning blessings soon after you awake. After that, you should immerse yourself in a mikveh (ritual bath), then put sackcloth around your waist, take a small pile of ashes and sit on the ground near a doorway. Then put some of the ashes on your forehead and start reciting a verse from the Tikkun Chatzot liturgy. Everyone is free to choose their own blessings and verse according to their own unique beliefs. The liturgy is also designed to get your soul closer to the divine presence, so choosing a verse you feel will take you closer to this goal is good. Each text is tied to a specific meditation exercise, and practitioners often choose according to the technique that helps them focus the most.

When you have finished studying the text, you may move on to reciting personal prayers, poems, and meditation. You can also immerse yourself into Kabbalah further studies and familiarize yourself with Zohar, Mishnah, or the Writings of Ari. All this will help you connect with the creator, and by strengthening your affinity to him, you will empower yourself to work towards a perfected state of mind.

Other Kaballistic Traditions

As mentioned before, mystics often prefer doing mindfulness exercises before performing any other Kabbalistic act. Everything can be incorporated into the rituals, from simple breathing techniques to meditation to passive exercise like yoga. Some of these can be performed during the act itself. For example, the technique of alternative counting meditation includes counting each night with a rosary while meditating on the Divine presence of Shekinah. The mystical acts related to the Tarot are discussed in several other chapters of this book.

Chapter 4: Depictions of the Tarot in the Tree of Life

So far, throughout this book, you've learned how Tarot is part of a unique, esoteric system that seamlessly weaves together the practice of Tarot with astrology and Kabbalah, contributing to a greater system of understanding ourselves and the world around us. This chapter will concentrate on the Tree of Life. We will study it to divulge its precise meaning and how it can be applied practically to the art of Tarot. A brief explanation would be that the Tree of Life symbolizes humanity's relationship with the Divine in the grand scheme of things. Because of its symbolic nature, we can easily use Tarot cards as a medium to safely and efficiently facilitate our understanding of life and our place within it.

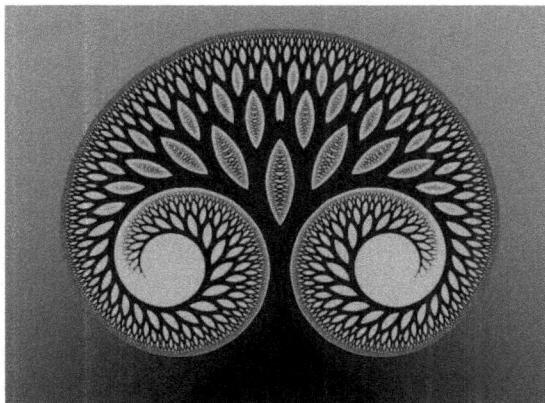

However, the practical application of this knowledge may feel a little abstract and confusing to you at the moment, which is understandable. The rest of this chapter will help illustrate how the Tarot and The Tree of Life are connected and the best ways for you to honor this spiritual divination in your daily life.

What Is the Tree of Life?

Before going into how the Tarot and our understanding of the Tree of Life can enhance our practice of Kabbalah, it is worth pausing to explain precisely what the Tree of Life is and what it represents symbolically. Simply put, the Tree of Life is a diagram that visually illustrates the laws of reality as they apply to our metaphysical realm. Like a fractal, the Tree of Life is an everlasting depiction of the divine principle, both as a microcosm and macrocosm. It resides within every one of us, and when we put humanity altogether, we form the branches of the tree.

This interconnectedness is further represented by the sinewy pathways running along every branch and all its roots, which illustrate how the spirit and our energy can travel to help make ourselves manifest in matter. If we are to follow the path of the Tree of Life downward, we will find other visual representations of our existence within this realm, such as the body and our subconscious. Further up the tree, we would find the divine source of the soul and our higher selves. Overall, the Tree of Life is recognized as the blueprint for creation, and it is a rich metaphor for the depth and complexity of our lives.

It is worth elaborating on the fact that the Tree of Life in Kabbalah possesses a ten sephirot structure, which is arranged in three pillars. The sephirot is basically a type of spiritual light that emanates from the aspect of the creator. It contains the laws governing the entirety of creation, so everything emanates from that base structure.

When illustrated diagrammatically, the Tree of Life will be shown to consist of ten different nodes and twenty-two paths that connect to each of them. How they communicate with one another reveals different things about ourselves, our relationship with those around us, and our destiny. The Tree of Life is a deeply complex subject within studies of the occult and Kabbalah, and there is a limit to which we can honor the intricate ins and outs within this chapter. In general, the discussion will focus strictly on applying the knowledge of the Tree of Life to our studies of Tarot and the best ways to enrich our understanding of the divine according to the skills at hand.

Understanding Connections

One useful thing to start with is illustrating precisely how the Tree of Life connects with the ten minor cards and how these, in turn, relate to the Sephira of the Tree. Each card signifies the end of a life cycle, event, or enterprise. They, in effect, represent both new beginnings and endings, indicating the circular nature of life. Each of the ten cards we will focus on here include the culmination of various life lessons and major milestones that can be dissected further to illuminate the user's point of view. So, without further ado, we will focus on the sephira that encapsulates the Tree of Life and pinpoint the unique characteristics of each one.

Keter

The Keter is the first Sephira. The name denotes "crown," which symbolizes the divine will of the Creator. It is the highest and most encompassing sephira in the Tree of Life since the crown is on the top of the head. In Tarot, it is typically represented in the Ace card, and the terms that most signify the Keter are "closest to god," "unity," "eternal source," "pureness," and "potential."

Furthermore, the Keter is rooted just above the Divine Nature of the Creator, making it incomprehensible to man. It is often posited in Kabbalah studies that this unknowable nature renders the will of the Creator as the most hidden of all the hidden things available to us in the universe. And, because the Keter represents perfection because of its proximity to the Creator, absolutely no flaw can exist in this sephira.

Hokma

Hokma is the second most important branch in the Tree of Life. It is on the uppermost right line of the sephirot and is traced directed to the Keter. The word is Hebrew for wisdom. Since it resides on the right line of the tree, it belongs to the Pillar of Mercy grouping of that sephirot.

In the Kabbalah tradition, the archangel Raziel is in charge of Hokma, and according to various theological texts, he is credited with writing the Book of Raziel the Angel. This pivotal work claims to explain all the divine secrets of both celestial and earthly worlds. In popular stories detailing the book's writing, it is said that Raziel stood close to God's throne, which allowed him to hear everything that was said. Raziel could then commit all the insights he had picked up to paper, and much of his writing was about creative energy, the intellectual process, and how they connect with the spiritual realm, culminating in action in the physical realm. The Book Raziel the Angel is regarded as one of the central texts of the Kabbalah religion, and devoted students review its many truths eagerly.

Hokma's dual nature is invoked through a multicolor card when it comes to the Tarot. Because it is seen as the central driver and sustainer of life, it is given an androgynous identity that veers toward the masculine side of the scale. Finally, the image behind the adage "let there be light" is seen to emerge from the Hokma, which further underscores its popular visual representation.

Binah

The third Sephir is Binah, which sits just below the Keter and across from the hokma.

Binah is Hebrew for "understanding," and the branch is located precisely on the left-hand side of the Sephirot. The Binah is considered to be the mirror image of the Hokomah. The former is a more intuitive understanding of the world via meditative contemplation, whereas the latter is the hard-earned and sought-after knowledge of the spiritual and physical planes. When combined, they help to give shape to the spirit of the Divine.

Another way in which Binah can be viewed as the mirror image of Hokma is that the former is often represented in feminine form, whereas the latter is primarily viewed as possessing masculine energy. In addition, Binah is often associated with the ethics of repentance, or an attempt to connect deeply with the Creator, thereby acknowledging one's own shortcomings in the understanding of the world's inner workings. The archangel Jehovah Elohim presides over Binah, and it is represented in the Tarot through the priestess card or associations with goddesses and important feminine figures such as Isis, Demeter, Juno, or The Virgin Mary.

Hesed

The fourth Sephir on the Tree of Life, located on the third branch on the right-hand side, is the Hesed. The word means "mercy" but is also referred to as "The Mighty One." The part of the Sephirot also relates to intellect, right before it dovetails into the tree's more emotive, emotional side. The archangel Zadkiel is associated with Hesed since he is the angel of mercy. Zadkiel's name is Hebrew for "righteousness of God," which is fitting since his role in scriptures – not to mention the role of this particular Sephir – is meant to reassure those who have done something wrong that forgiveness can be found. God cares and is merciful to them, provided that they confess and repent their sins. This is the role that Zadkiel plays since he encourages people to seek the forgiveness that the Creator generously offers, regardless of how hurt or aggrieved they may feel. This Sephir is also considered to be especially powerful for its capacity to heal emotional scars and rid people of their painful memories.

Hesed is associated with the principles of love and kindness and, as mentioned above, represents the connection between the intellectual and more emotive attributes of the Sephirot. In Tarot, Hesed is represented by the element of water, and an ethereal figure of some kind, often shown as a king seated on a sapphire throne. Other symbols include a horse, unicorn, orb or wand, and a scepter.

Geburah

Geburah is the fifth Ssephir in the Tree of Life, three branches down from Keter and to the left-hand side of the Sephirot. Geburah means "strength" and, in more general terms, is used to represent the "Almighty." The archangel of Ggeburah is Camiel, who is also known as the angel of peaceful relationships. People are encouraged to turn to Camiel when they search for unconditional love or need to find inner peace. They also draw strength from the archangel's capacity to resolve conflicts and to forgive those who have hurt them. Geburah is the Sephir for harmony and grants people the strength to overcome obstacles and connect on a deeper level. Most visual representations in Tarot consist of a heart since

Geburah also represents love, and the vibrant colors of pink and red more closely resemble its intense energy.

Tiphareth

Tiphareth is at the center of the Tree of Life. It is the beating heart that connects all branches. It is also the sixth Sephirot. The word Tiphareth is Hebrew for "beauty," and the Sephir is referred to as "God Manifest" in theological texts. The Tiphareth is represented by the archangel Raphael who works to heal the deep-seated physical pain we feel due to emotional pain. Since this Sephir connects all the different branches of the tree together – the emotional, intellectual, and physical aspects – it works to create spiritual and physical autonomy. Since the body, mind, and spirit are intricately connected and work together as a whole, any stressors or feelings of fear you experience will affect you and may manifest themselves as a physical injury. Therefore, we can revert to Tiphareth and Archangel Raphael whenever we need healing. In tarot, the cards representing science, pleasure, or victory correspond to the Tiphareth.

Netzach

The seventh branch located toward the bottom of the Tree of Life, to the right side of the Sephirot, Netzach, is Hebrew for "Eternity" and is also sometimes referred to as the "Lord of Hosts." The archangel Jehovah Sabaoth is thought to be the progenitor of this concept of eternity. Given the Netzach's position within the Tree of Life (it lies directly at the base of the aforementioned "Pillar of Mercy," located right under Chesed and Hokma), in the context of Kabbalah, Netzach refers to victory and endurance, as well as to infinity.

The Netzach is also part of the Sephirah that is related to intuition, sensitivity, and feelings. Its visual representation in Tarot attributes it to the forces of nature, with the colors blue, gold, olive, and emerald green used to connote its aura.

Hod

The eighth branch on the left side of the Tree of Life, Hod, is Hebrew for glory. The archangel Raphael is associated with this Sephir, and he is usually referred to as the angel of healing. The Hod is also the "God of Hosts" in Kabbalah since it has four paths to the other major Sephirs; Tiphereth, Netzach, Hesed, and Geburah. The Hod is described as a force that helps break energy down into different forms. It is mostly associated with the intellectual arm of the Sephirot, embodying learning and ritual. On the opposite end is the Netzach Sephir, a power of energy used to overcome barriers and limitations. It is also associated with emotions, passion, music, and dancing.

Yesod

Yesod is the ninth branch residing in the Tree of Life center. The word means "the foundation" in Hebrew and is also referred to as the "Mighty Living One." The Yesod is represented by the archangel Gabriel, who is considered to be the patron saint of communication since he is God's top messenger. Across the different monotheistic religions, the angel Gabriel is shown delivering important messages from God to humanity, which is why people are encouraged to pray to him when they need to connect to others or seek information.

Within the context of the Kabbalah, Yesod is essentially the foundation on which the Creator built the world. This Sephir also serves as the transmitter between the Sephiras right above it and the reality vectors just below it. Because of this, Yesod is also considered to be the conduit of sexual energy, allowing humans to communicate with earth, thereby interacting with divinity. The unifying power of the Yesod is mostly captured through the vibrant colors of purple, indigo, and violet.

Malkuth

The Malkuth is the tenth Sephir in the Tree of Life, located at the very bottom, acting as a counterpoint to the Keter, which is located at the crown. Malkuth is Hebrew for "the kingdom" and is also called "Lord of Earth." The archangel Sandalphon is the angel who cares for the earth and is present to hear the people's prayers to God and work to direct the music in heaven. Some theological experts believe Sandalphon to have been the prophet Elijah before he became an angel. He is seen as inspiring people to praise God in creative ways since there is a part of his central essence that is connected to the earth like humans.

In Kabbalah, the Malkuth is considered to be the final phase of active manifestation. Because of this Sephir, we are grounded in the physical realm and continue going about our daily lives, all the while looking up to the other branches in the Tree of Life. All spiritual exercises are rooted and secured in the Malkuth, and it would be impossible to connect with other realms without first acknowledging the presence of the earth's foundation. In Tarot, the cards Ten of Cups, Ten of Swords, and Ten of Wands belong to this Sephir and express much of what can occur in the Malkuth.

Meditative Practices and the Tree of Life

There are several ways to meditate within the kabbalah tradition, using the Sephirot as a guide. No one way can be singled out as being the be-all and end of all, but there are a few popular meditations that practitioners can do that focus on invoking the divine names of the Sephirs. Usually, the meditation will consist of repeating the names of each Sephir, alternating with a sequence of Hebrew letters. This practice helps to center the spirit and teaches the individual to try different breathing techniques.

The best way to do this meditation is to repeat the divine name of each Sephir – the Malkuth, Keter, Yesod, Geburah, and so on – followed by the incantation of several Hebrew letters. Pause every once in a while to try various breathing styles, and you will notice that the interpretation of whatever happens in the body or mind during the meditation will vary over time. Sometimes this meditation will help calm the mind, relieve stress, and allow the individual to feel and experience the Divine. For others, it may produce a calming effect on the physical symptoms of anxiety, allowing you a chance to slow down a bit and have a chance to contemplate the secrets of the spiritual realm.

Practitioners of Kabbalah attribute a great deal of spiritual development to recitations of the holy names and seeing and keeping the Tree of Life in your mind's eye. While some of the meditative practices are highly intellectualized in Kabbalah, it is entirely possible to freeform the tradition and create something unique to you, provided, of course, that you fully understand the Tree of Life and the intricate history of each of the vital branches and their place within the religion.

Creative Energies and the Tree of Life

In summary, the Tree of Life illustrates how the Creator can express its creative energy throughout the universe, through angels first and then human beings. Each of the tree's branches – or Sephir – symbolizes a vital creative force that a singular archangel oversees. Followers of this belief system believe deeply that focusing on one of these energies at a time will allow people to develop a closer spiritual union with the Divine and will provide a closer look into how some of the more mysterious aspects of the universe operate. Then, the meditative practice can be deepened by reminding yourself of the singular nature of each of the branches and their relationship to a metaphysical or spiritual plane. Of course, Tarot in Kabbalah plays a central role in these meditative practices, involving settling the mind and visualization. This understanding, once mastered, will provide a wealth of healing that can be especially powerful during difficult times.

Chapter 5: Interpreting the Major Arcana

In Kabbalah, the collective path of Major Arcana is also known as The Fool's Journey, which illustrates the descent into Malkut and the continuation of one's path toward the light. Each of the 22 paths of the Major Arcana is linked to a letter in the Hebrew alphabet, and each of these letters gives deeper meaning to the cards.

This chapter will go through the individual cards, describing each of their detailed Kabbalistic interpretations, and provide you with a better understanding of how they are related to the Journey of The Fool. Working with the Major Arcana combined with the Kabbalistic Tree of Life gives you a deeper insight into who and what the Fool is and how the journey is accomplished. In the beginning, The Fool is depicted as a raw form of energy. As it goes through each path of the Major Arcana, it transforms until it reaches its full potential. And just The Fool cannot skip any parts of its journey, neither can you. To develop a higher sense of spirituality and evolve into the best version of yourself – you must follow the pathways from one Sephira to the next one.

The Fool

Letter: א (Aleph)

Path: Kether (Crown) – Chokmah (Wisdom)

Element: Air

The Fool card illustrates a young person taking their first steps into the world. They are walking without care, carrying a small sack, and unwittingly heading toward a cliff, where they will encounter their first hurdle in life. In their exuberant joy, they don't even notice the threat, or if they do, they aren't concerned with it. Their only chance of avoiding the danger is paying attention to the dog barking at their feet, trying to make them aware of their surroundings.

In Kabbalah, this card is seen as a symbol of childlike spirituality and teaches you how to incorporate positivity into your consciousness, regardless of the difficulties you may be facing. The Fool also corresponds to the Kabbalistic number zero – which represents the balance of all opposites. By consulting this card during meditation, you can reach a state of consciousness where all your thoughts will be united and the harmony between negative and positive restored. If you can only spare a few minutes daily to meditate on the Fool, you'll find that everything will seem brighter.

The Magician

Letter: ב (Beth)

Path: Kether (Crown) – Binah (Understanding)

Element: Air

The Magician card shows a central figure pointing to the sky with one hand and to the ground with the other. This symbolizes their ability to interpret messages from the human world and those above it. In front of him are the four Tarot suits, showing that the Magician works with the four cardinal elements. It could indicate that he has to put his mind, body, soul, and heart into everything he does. The infinity symbol on the figure's head indicates the infinite outcomes possible, created through the Magician's will.

THE MAGICIAN.

The Magician Tarot card shows you that you are in control of your destiny. Its Kabbalistic reference is to the highest energy in nature – which is the one that comes from your own willpower. So, if you need guidance on how to improve yourself, meditating on the Magician will show you the way. Before you rush to make any decisions, you should always practice self-discipline, and your dreams will come true without too many mishaps along the way.

The High Priestess

Letter: ג (Gimel)

Path: Kether (Crown) – Tiphareth (Beauty)

Element: Water

The High Priestess is shown sitting on a stone between two pillars of Solomon's Temple – the Pillar of Strength and the Pillar of Establishment. She also represents the third pillar, the path between the two major facets of reality. On her head sits the crown of Isis, indicating her aptitude for magic, while the solar cross she wears as a talisman shows her affinity for nature. She also has a crescent moon at her feet, meaning she has control over her emotions.

The Kabbalistic interpretation of the High Priestess card identifies it as the representation of spirituality and understanding. It is used to teach you that you must let go of your fears if you want to reach your goals. Sometimes fears prevent you from following your intuition. At other times, it can bring out your insecurities. You can learn to balance your emotions and strengths by focusing on the card during meditation. Just visualize yourself between the path of love you must embrace and the path of logic – and make a commitment to respect both.

The Empress

Letter: ד (Daleth)

Path: Chokmah (Wisdom) – Binah (Understanding)

Element: Earth

The Empress card depicts the goddess of fertility sitting on her throne, ready to attend to those needing her help. Her expression is gentle, just as a protective mother should be. She is surrounded by a riot of colorful, natural elements, including an enchanting green forest and a refreshingly pure river. Her blond hair is adorned with stars, symbolic of the great mystical power she yields in the universe. Her pomegranate-patterned robe and cushions embroidered with venous signs illustrate her association with fertility.

Not only does the Empress card symbolize your inner mother figure, but it also shows how we express the wisdom we receive through her. While Kabbalah emphasizes a healthy dose of self-criticism, the Empress will often show your inner mother's negative impact on your thoughts and emotions. If you want to find out what lurks beneath your conscious mind, meditate with the card just as the Empress does – sitting in nature and using its healing power.

The Emperor

Letter: ה (He)

Path: Chokmah (Wisdom) – Tiphareth (Beauty)

Element: Fire

The Emperor card shows a stoic authority figure who is sitting on a throne embellished with the heads of four rams. He has a scepter and an orb in his hands, representing his right to rule and the kingdom he oversees. The Emperor has a long beard, the sign of his infinite wisdom. His ambition, determination, and pure strength he exudes are shown in the barren mountains behind him. The Emperor balances out the power of the Empress by bringing law and order to her unstructured, natural kingdom.

The Emperor can teach you about the positive elements of life – as long as you are sensibly approaching them. You will find his influence in every concrete action you take and every tangible result you achieve. He can also warn you against being inflexible or ignoring your needs, so it's good to heed his advice in organizing your life. Kabbalistic meditation with the card is a great way to receive guidance from the great ruler or plan ahead and establish a well-organized life.

The Hierophant

Letter: ו (Vau)

Path: Chokmah (Wisdom) – Chesed (Mercy)

Element: Earth

This card shows a religious figure sitting in an environment resembling traditional religious monuments. The three vestments the figure wears represent three worlds, while the horizontal bars in the triple cross he is carrying in his left hand denote the Father, the Son, and the Holy Spirit. The Hierophant`s right hand is raised to bless the acolytes sitting in front of him after empowering them with his wisdom and spiritual beliefs.

In Kabbalah, the Hierophant represents the card dealing with spiritual issues, often within entire communities. It points out that it is always easier for a group of people will achieve a greater good than individuals and urges you to connect with those around you. If you aren't sure how to reach out to your community, you should try meditating with this card and ask the Hierophant to mentor you, just as he does with all his students. He will show you how to accept other people's beliefs while still honoring your traditional beliefs.

The Lovers

Letter: ז (Zayin)

Path: Binah (Understanding) – Tiphareth (Beauty)

Element: Air

The Lovers Tarot card depicts a man and a woman being protected by the angel Raphael, who hovers above them. The couple represents the union of two opposing forces. Their home is the Garden of Eden, which is illustrated by a fruit tree and a snake behind the woman. Their guardian angel maintains the harmony in the couple's life, preventing them from yielding to temptations all around them and blessing them with the ability to form a healthy relationship.

THE LOVERS.

The Lovers card prompts you to look behind the souls of two people in each relationship. Acknowledging the third soul – the soul of your relationship, is fundamental for every union, as it allows you to understand the purpose of the relationship. People often fail to recognize this soul, hindering the opportunity to deepen their relationships. Kabbalistic meditations focusing on the Lovers card and the other party will show you how to communicate with the soul of your relationship and reveal all the secrets preventing you from moving forward.

The Chariot

Letter: ח (Chet)

Path: Binah (Understanding) – Geburah (Severity)

Element: Water

This card shows a figure sitting in a vehicle with blue upholstery adorned with white stars. The vehicle is driven by two sphinxes, colored black and white, to symbolize the opposing forces their owner must dominate. The owner has a sign of a crescent moon on his shoulder, representing his spiritual guide. The crown on his head symbolizes his power. On his chest, a square denotes the earth on which he is grounded.

While the animals seem calm on the card, they can easily go wild, wanting to go in several different directions, just like human emotions. You must learn how to contain them, but not so much that you can't express them. They are the emotions that motivate you to work toward success. Focusing on the Chariot card during meditation will help you find the balance between expressing your passion and letting your emotions run wild. It can also show you new possibilities and further inspire you.

The Strength

Letter: ט (Tet)

Path: Geburah (Severity) – Tiphareth (Beauty)

Element: Fire

This tarot card depicts a woman holding the jaws of a lion. Despite the animal's obvious threat, the woman shows no signs of fear. Not only does she have the courage to keep the lion at bay, but she can control the animal gracefully, without hurting it. The lion in itself is a symbol of great courage. The mountains with the blue sky above them in the background testify to the strength and stability it takes to remain courageous.

Remaining calm and disciplined is especially important in times of great adversity – otherwise, your feelings can lead you to your destruction. While a healthy dose of courage and dynamic strength are necessary qualities, you mustn't forget the principle of mind over matter. According to Kabbalah, only those who influence their own passion can progress toward the union with the divine. Meditation with the Strength card is particularly helpful in balancing creative and rational forces.

The Hermit

Letter: י (Yod)

Path: Chesed (Mercy) – Tiphareth (Beauty)

Element: Earth

The Hermit card shows an older man standing at a mountain peak. He looks committed to his path and wields authority with the staff held in one of his hands. On the other, he has a lantern, a sign of his ability to impart knowledge. His position speaks of the success, accomplishment, and spiritual knowledge he has gained over the years. Inside the lantern is the Seal of Solomon, a hallmark of infinite understanding.

In Kabbalah, the Hermit card represents finding the key to personal development or a secret hidden deep inside your soul. It emphasizes the importance of true values in life rather than focusing on materialistic goals. It is best used in meditation performed in solitude and repeated several times throughout an extended period. Remember, the answers to all fundamental questions always come from within. Taking the time to unveil all the answers will be worth it as this will allow you to satisfy your inner desires.

The Wheel of Fortune

Letter: כ (Kaph)

Path: Chesed (Mercy) – Netzach (Victory)

Element: Fire

On this card, a large wheel is depicted as being surrounded by an angel, a lion, an eagle, and a bull. These creatures are all adorned with wings, while the wheel is covered in esoteric symbols. Each creature holds a book, symbolizing their eagerness to adopt the wisdom of the Torah. A sphinx sits on top of the wheel, and an evil figure is seen underneath it. These are the two opposing forces that take turns ruling the world as the wheel turns.

The Wheel of Fortune card clearly shows that while there will always be difficulties, they are always followed by a reward. According to Kabbalah, overcoming hurdles is a practice that leads to a higher spiritual essence. The spokes on the wheel represent the directions to your innermost desires, whose fulfillment causes joy. Therefore, following them is essential to obtain happiness, and even more so in difficult times when you need added motivation to move on with your life.

The Justice

Letter: ל (Lamed)

Path: Geburah (Severity) – Chesed (Mercy)

Element: Air

The Justice card illustrates a figure sitting in their chair and holding scales in her left hand. The scales depict the balance between logic and inner guide, but the figure also shows fairness by holding an upright sword in their other hand.

The clarity of Justice is further emphasized by the crown and the purple cloak depicted on the card. The white shoe peeking out from beneath the cloak reminds us that all actions have consequences, no matter how much we try to hide them.

This card points out the importance of fairness in justice. Depending on your actions, everything can be resolved for or against you, and the outcome may not be what you have desired. But after all, the divine is about being just, even if you can't see it yet. Meditation or journeying while contemplating both sides of your actions will help you come to terms with the negative consequences. Over time, you will learn to accept to endure hardship, knowing there are better times to come.

The Hanged Man

Letter: מ (Mem)

Path: Geburah (Severity) – Hod (Splendor)

Element: Water

This card depicts a man in an upside-down position. He is suspended by his right foot and is hanging from a living world tree, rooted in the underworld. The man has a calm expression as if he chooses to be in this position. He also has a bright halo around his head – indicating his enlightened state. The man's body resembles an inverted triangle, as his left foot is free, but both his hands are secured behind his back. The colors of his clothes, pants being red and shirt being blue, denotes the balance between passion and calm emotions.

The Hanging Man shows that acting purely based on passion is not always the best idea during challenging times. Instead of instinctively trying to free yourself from whatever situation you have found yourself in, you should first focus on gathering your strength. It can teach you how to transcend pain and send a powerful message to your inner, fierce self – something that will bring you closer to union with the creator.

The Death

Letter: נ (Nun)

Path: Tiphareth (Beauty) – Netzach (Victory)

Element: Water

On this tarot card, Death is shown as a living skeleton, which portrays the only part left of the human body after death. The skeleton is riding a white horse and holds a black flag with white markings. By wearing the armor, Death is depicted as invincible. The horse symbolizes purity because Death erases everything. The masses beneath him consist of many different shapes and sizes, showing that Death does not differentiate between gender, race, or class.

The Death card is usually associated with negative change. However, according to the Kabbalah, Death may bring other changes that might be favorable for you – but sometimes, not for others. Still, this shouldn't deter you from seeking them out because sooner or later, you will encounter those that see this change in the same light as you do. As long as they shepherd you toward becoming a healthier, more spiritually balanced version of yourself, you have nothing to lose from your changes.

The Temperance

Letter: ס (Samech)

Path: Tiphareth (Beauty) – Yesod (Foundation)

Element: Fire

The Temperance card shows an angel with one foot in the water, representing the world's natural side. Its other leg is on dry land, depicting the world's materialistic aspect. The angel is wearing a robe, on which there is a triangle, alluding to the holy trinity. The angel is also holding two cups of water, mixing them, and letting the water flow back and forth, just as the infinite life cycle does.

In Kabbalah, the Temperance card advises you to sacrifice your ego – that is, if you want to restore your connection to the natural cycle of life. Everything can be used for dual purposes, and the key is to use them as a tool instead of a weapon. This often means lots of practice and prolonged meditation sessions, as finding your ego means unearthing a lost aspect of yourself. Still, everyone has their own guardian angel, and if you listen to it, you will receive the message that takes you forward in life.

The Devil

Letter: ע (Ayin)

Path: Tiphareth (Beauty) – Hod (Splendor)

Element: Earth

The card depicts the Devil as a human being with goat-like features, horns, and bat wings. Between his eyes, he has an inverted pentagram. A man and a woman are shackled to the platform that the Devil is sitting on, giving the impression that he is holding them captive. Under his dominion, both the man and the woman have developed horns, becoming less human. While both of them are addicted to having riches, none of it makes them happy as their free will is taken away from them.

Over time, we develop subconscious coping mechanisms which guide us to navigate our relationships with everyone and everything around us. Unfortunately, not all of them are healthy, and sometimes they force us to make decisions against our true desires. To avoid this inner struggle, and develop healthier relationships, try meditating on factors that keep the Devil on your side. Uncovering this secret will allow you to break free of your chains and bring you closer to the divine.

The Tower

Letter: פ (Phe)

Path: Hod (Splendor) - Netzach (Victory)

Element: Fire

This card illustrates a tower set high on top of the mountain - at the exact moment, it is set ablaze by a lightning bolt. As the flames are devouring the building, people are jumping out of its windows in a desperate attempt to save their lives - symbolizing our need to escape our inner turmoil. Still, their endeavor is based upon a faulty premise, which is their destruction and that of the tower's - which is inevitable.

Just as the destruction of the tower can't be avoided, neither can the consequences of negative thoughts, emotions, and actions. Everything based on these characteristics must be destroyed before you can move toward rebuilding a new life. Through Kabbalistic meditation, the Tower card will teach you the importance of flexibility. So, when you are struggling with repressed emotions, you will be reminded that the lowest points in the Tree of Life are there to deal with the toughest things in life. Doing so will help you adjust to the daily changes.

The Star

Letter: צ (Tzaddi)

Path: Netzach (Victory) – Yesod (Foundation)

Element: Air

The Star card depicts a woman kneeling at a small pond, holding two buckets full of water. One of them is tilted, and the water starts to spill, nourishing the lush, green earth. The woman has one foot in the pond, indicating her spiritual abilities, while the other is kept firmly on the ground, showing her strength. A bird on the tree branch beside the woman also illustrates sacred wisdom.

THE STAR.

According to Kabbalah, expanding your consciousness will take your state of mind and spirit to a higher level. The Star tarot card indicates that this state may already be in sight – you just have to work for it. Meditation is the best way to nurture your consciousness so you can manifest a brighter future. It helps you focus on being grounded to set up constructive goals and develop compassion toward yourself and others without losing sight of your ultimate reward.

The Moon

Letter: ק (Quoph)

Path: Netzach (Victory) – Malkuth (Kingdom)

Element: Water

The Moon card shows a picture that depicts a path leading into the far distance. On either side of the path are two animals, both of which represent the animalistic nature of living beings. The tamed dog on one side and the feral wolf on the other emphasize the dualism within this nature. The trail starts from a pond, out of which a crawfish is emerging, and there are two towers that flank the path, which alludes to the opposing forces of good and evil.

Just as the Moon has two phases, waxing and waning, we also have two main phases in life. Our life path is a paradoxical journey between positive and negative energies. Ultimately, there are only these two possibilities to choose from, no matter how your path is shaped. It's also full of ups and downs depending on the force you allow to take over your path. Using the Moon card for meditation during the waxing phase promotes personal growth, but in the waning phase, it can cause hindrance.

The Sun

Letter: ר (Resh)

Path: Hod (Splendor) – Yesod (Foundation)

Element: Fire

This card shows the Sun rising and bringing brightness after the dark hours of the night. As the Sun is the source of life on Earth, it brings optimism and renewed energy at dawn. A child is playing joyfully in front of the Sun, who is shown to be the picture of innocence. The child is naked, indicating they have nothing to hide and is as innocent and pure as possible. The horse, the child, is riding is another illustration of this.

THE SUN .

One can only be as happy and confident as the Sun card's child if you are truly aligned with yourself. While the card can promise you glory and fortune, true fulfillment can only come from what you truly desire, such as health in mind and body. Meditate using the Sun card at dawn to avoid being caught in the darkness of vanity and thinking you only need material riches. It will bring you the success you seek without sacrificing the brightness in other areas of life.

The Judgment

Letter: ש (Shin)

Path: Hod (Splendor) – Malkuth (Kingdom)

Element: Fire

The Judgment Tarot Card shows illustrations of various figures awaiting their final judgment after death. Their spiritual forms are pictured rising from their graves and standing in front of Gabriel, calling them one by one. Their arms are outstretched, ready to receive whatever verdict the universe is about to impose upon them. Whether it's hell or heaven, they have already accepted their fate. Behind the figures is a menacing tidal wave, further emphasizing the sheer inevitability of the final judgment.

According to the Kabbalah, this universe will propel you forward towards your destiny no matter what. Whether under the influence of other people, or outside circumstances, your fate can take you in many different directions. Despite this, you also have the power to change course and head wherever you want to go. The Judgment card can help you manifest a mystical coincidence that pushes you in the right direction. Meditation with outstretched hands will allow you to hear the universe's call and act accordingly.

The World

Letter: ת (Tav)

Path: Yesod (Foundation) – Malkuth (Kingdom)

Element: Earth

The World card shows a central dancing figure surrounded by a green wreath of flowers and red ribbons. Apart from showing off a person's success in life, the wreath is also associated with infinity or the divine state of being. One of the figure's legs is crossed over the other, and they have a wand in each hand – symbolizing the balance between static and constant evolution of the moment. There are also four smaller figures at each corner of the card, representing the four corners of the universe.

In Kabbalah, the World card typically points to the cycle of life, emphasizing that from beginning to end, humans have only one goal – and that is to unite with the creator. It can also be understood as the balance between perfection and the imperfection of the universe. If used for reflection, it also reveals a similar balance within yourself. Regular meditation with the card while focusing on this harmony leads to self-realization in your divine self.

Chapter 6: Interpreting the Minor Arcana

The Minor Arcana Cards are more attuned with the physical world (the world that surrounds us) and consist of planets and stars. They show you practical aspects of what we call the material plane. Therefore, you will find it easier to become attuned to them throughout your professional and personal life. Tarot's Minor Arcana consists of 56 cards, split into four suits of fourteen cards: Wands, Cups, Swords, and Pentacles. Like in a regular deck of playing cards, each suit consists of cards numbered one (Ace) to ten, and the four Court Cards; Page, Knight, Queen, and King. These cards also correspond to the four elements (air, water, fire, and earth) and four yetziratic (Kabbalistic) worlds.

Wands

The suit of Wands is associated with the Hebrew letter ׳ (Yod), the fire element and Atziluth, the World of Emanation, and the divine Faculty of Intuition.

Ace of Wands

This card is illustrated with a hand reaching out from a cloud while holding a still wand which is still growing. You can see this in the sprouting leaves, representing spiritual and material progress. You can also see a castle, which is symbolic of all the wonderful opportunities available in the future – calling out to you to follow your dreams. The Ace of Wands tells you that any great idea you've come up with recently is worth following.

Two of Wands

This card portrays a man standing on top of a castle with a globe in his right hand. He is looking down on an ocean on the left side and solid land on the right side, contemplating how to expand his life experiences. His red hat shows he is ready for adventure, and his orange tunic signifies his enthusiasm. The Two of Wands points out the importance of planning for progression.

Three of Wands

This card illustrates a man standing on the edge of a cliff, with wands planted in the ground all around him. As he looks over the ocean and the mountains, he grabs a wand in his hand. He seems to reflect on the commitment to his plans and how to make them become a reality. The Three of Wands hints that you are on the right path by creating a stable foundation for your plans.

Four of Wands

This card depicts a couple dancing beneath a wreath tied between four crystal-tipped wands. There is also a canopy of flowers characteristic of traditional Jewish wedding ceremonies, symbolizing the couple's celebration. The Four of Wands reflects the expectation of joyous family holidays. It also signals the importance of meeting personal goals – another achievement that brings satisfaction and fulfillment to your life.

Five of Wands

In this card, you can see five men thrusting their wands upwards as if they are in disagreement with each other. However, they seem relaxed, which means that their rivalry is good-natured and not fueled by anger towards each other. The Five of Wands encourages you to accept your competition as a means to improve yourself, rather than looking at them as if they were people wanting to hurt you.

Six of Wands

The card depicts a man riding a horse through a crowd of cheering people, wearing a wreath of victory on his head. Both this and the wreath tied to the wand he is carrying further emphasize the acknowledgment of his accomplishments. His horse is white, symbolizing his purity and power, and victory. The Six of Wands indicates success in expressing your talents and ensuring the completion of goals.

Seven of Wands

This card shows a man standing on top of a hill, defending himself from his opponents who are challenging him from below. The man is not wearing matching shoes, indicating that he is on uneven ground or doesn't have a stable footing in life. The Seven of Wands means that as long as you can hold your ground, you will defend your position, no matter what your opponents are challenging you with.

Eight of Wands

This card displays eight flying wands traveling through the air. Some have blossoms on them and are still traveling at a maximum speed, while others seem to be near their destination, signaling the end of a long journey. The landscape shows an unclouded sky, which indicates that there is nothing in the way of those still searching for their destination. The Eight of Wands is a prophet of important news or a possibility for sudden growth.

Nine of Wands

This card shows a man holding on to a wand with eight other wands standing behind him. The man seems weak or injured yet still has a strong desire to fight another battle if needed. He looks hopeful and determined to get through whatever challenge lies ahead of him. The Nine of Wands symbolizes your life as a combination of challenges, victories, hope, and willingness to fight your battles.

Ten of Wands

On this card, a man is approaching a nearby town. He is carrying a bundle of ten wands in his hands, indicating his struggles in life, his success in overcoming them, and his reward for his victories. Nearing his destination, he is looking for a place to relax to revel in his success. The Ten of Wands indicates that you have a lot of responsibilities to fulfill before you can enjoy your victory.

Page of Wands

This card shows a well-dressed man standing on barren land, which indicates the fruitlessness of his world. He is holding a wand and seems passionate about his ideas, though these are still very hypothetical. However, the pattern of his shirt seems to change in fabric, symbolizing the transformation from bad to good. The Page of Wands inspires you to use your ideas and make discoveries to move forward in life.

Knight of Wands

A knight is sitting on a horse on this card, prepared to lunge into action. His yellow shirt, the plume sticking out of his helmet, and the orange color of his horse all speak about the fire he will be putting into winning his battles. He is fighting with a wand instead of a sword, indicating he will use lots of creativity. The Knight of Wands prompts you to place as much enthusiasm as you can into your creative projects.

Queen of Wands

This card depicts a queen sitting on her throne, holding a sunflower in her left hand and a blossoming wand in her right one, indicating that she brings warmth, fertility, and joy into the world. She is facing forward, showing her strength and determination to succeed. The Queen of Wands card signifies positive energy and the people who will always stand up for you when you need them.

King of Wands

This card depicts a king with a blossoming wand, demonstrating his passion for life and creativity. His orange cape and throne are embellished with salamanders and lions, which symbolize his strength and wit. The salamanders are biting their tails, which presents the image of an infinity sign, which means that he will always face obstacles along his way in life. The King of Wands encourages you to take on roles of which you are capable.

Cups

The suit of Cups is associated with the Hebrew letter ה (He), the water element and Beri'ah, the World of Creation, and the spiritual Faculty of Feeling.

Ace of Cups

A hand emerges from the clouds holding out a cup overflowing with water on this card. Five streams are pouring from the cup, indicating inner purity and the importance of listening to your inner voice. The Ace of Cups offers a deep sense of spiritual fulfillment to those willing to tap into their intuition and disregard other emotions caused by outside factors, regardless of their situation.

Two of Cups

This card depicts a man and a woman exchanging their cups to celebrate becoming one. The symbol of Hermes' caduceus between them indicates that they will need to negotiate and trade energy and protect and respect each other to have a successful union. Above it, there is a chimera, symbolizing the passion governing their relationship. The Two of Cups points out all the elements all new relationships need.

Three of Cups

This card shows you three women lifting their cups in a celebration, smiling at each other – a picture of beauty and happiness. They are standing on top of a vast field full of flowers and fruit. Their heads are adorned with wreaths made of flowers, further symbolizing their victory. The Three of Cups urges you to spend more quality time with those you cherish and who bring joy to your life.

Four of Cups

The card depicts a man sitting under a tree on a mountaintop, apparently contemplating his life. His hands and legs are crossed, and he is looking down at three cups in front of him, unaware of a fourth cup being presented in the air. His position represents our tendency to seek new treasures while taking whatever we already have for granted. The Four of Cups indicates that you sometimes aren't aware of what's happening.

Five of Cups

This card is illustrated with a man wearing a black cloak. Three cups toppled over on the ground, and he is mourning them. He doesn't even notice the other two cups standing on the ground. Behind him, a river separates him from a castle, symbolizing the conflicting emotions he may be dealing with. The Five of Cups indicates that you are stuck dwelling on your past regrets instead of moving forward with your life.

Six of Cups

Children are playing with six cups filled with white flowers on the card. In the foreground, a boy is passing a cup to a girl, symbolizing nostalgia and the celebration of reunions. The children are in a castle, which means they are protected and have all the security and comfort they need. The Six of Cups often indicates your need to seek comfort from those who love you unconditionally.

Seven of Cups

This card shows a person watching images emerging from the seven cups floating in the clouds – representing his dreams, illusions, and thoughts. Only the person's back is visible, which means he is either busy with wishful thinking or asleep, and we see the dreams he is conjuring up. The Seven of Cups implies that although you have several options, you will need to sort them out to make the best choice.

Eight of Cups

A cloaked figure on this card with eight golden cups behind him. He is heading off to barren, mountainous land, seeking a higher purpose, the excitement of the unknown, or new challenges. His ability to leave the cups he has collected behind speaks of his willingness to detach himself from others and his tendency for self-improvement. The Eight of Cups indicates that you must step away from familiar settings to grow spiritually.

Nine of Cups

This card shows a middle-aged man sitting on a wooden bench with his arms crossed and contentment on his face. He has a red headdress on, indicating he has an active mind. There are nine cups behind him, arranged in order, demonstrating that the man has achieved fulfillment and success in his life. The Nine of Cups indicates the happiness and satisfaction caused by fulfilling your innermost desires.

Ten of Cups

This card depicts a couple in a loving embrace, facing a vast green garden with a house. There are two children playing beside the couple, portraying that the couple is both materially and spiritually blessed. The ten cups form an arc above them, implying the blessings come from heaven. The river beside the home shows how freely love flows between individuals. The Ten of Cups sends a message of true emotional fulfillment.

Page of Cups

This card depicts a young woman wearing a blue tunic with a floral pattern and a long scarf near the seashore. She has a golden cup in her hand, but she looks at the fish coming out of the sea and staring expectantly at her. The Page of Cups inspires you to look into your intuition, reveal your dreams, and work persistently on making them come true – even if you don't understand their meaning yet.

Knight of Cups

This card depicts a young knight sitting on a white horse, holding a cup – as if he is carrying a message. The white horse symbolizes spirituality and immense power that comes from pure sources. Despite this, he has a look of serenity on his face, which means he has no intention to rush ahead but moves with caution. The Knight of Cups typically carries a message about the arrival of good fortune.

Queen of Cups

This card presents a queen sitting on her throne at the ocean's edge, signifying that her power lies between the fluid realm of emotions and the solid ground of thoughts. Since her feet aren't touching either world, she can look at her thoughts and emotions from the outside. She is focused on the closed cup she is holding. The Queen of Cups signals that you have to trust your inner voice.

King of Cups

A king seated on a throne with calm water surrounding him is the illustration for the King of Cups. He has a fish-shaped amulet on his necklace, representing his creative spirit. There are also fish in the ocean on the king's left side, while on his right, there is a ship, symbolizing the material world. The King of Cups teaches you to balance your impulses with your rationale rather than suppressing your intuition completely.

Swords

The suit of Swords is associated with the Hebrew letter ו (Vau), the element of air and Yetzirah, the World of Formation, and the psychical Faculty of Thinking.

ACE of SWORDS.

Ace of Swords

This card depicts a hand emerging from the clouds holding a double-edged sword adorned with a crown and a wreath associated with power, victory, and success. In the background, multiple other swords are floating over mountains and seas, symbolizing the vast territory they can conquer. The Ace of Swords indicates that you will experience a victorious breakthrough.

Two of Swords

The card illustrates a woman sitting and holding a sword in each hand. Behind her, vessels and ships are battling their way amongst the rocks in the sea. However, the woman is blindfolded, so she can't see the problem or its resolution. The Two of Swords indicates that there are often two very different solutions to our issues. Before making a decision, you must consider both of them, even if neither of them seems too appealing.

Three of Swords

This card displays a floating heart pierced by three swords. Above it, heavy clouds are causing a heavy downpour, indicating that all actions can have immediate effects. The three swords are causing grief, pain, and suffering, displacing the sensation of warmth, affection, and contentment that the heart feels when it's whole. The Three of Swords signifies that you are at the lowest point of your life, and you must decide whether or not you will stay there.

Four of Swords

This card is illustrated by a carving of a praying knight on a tomb in a church. He has a sword beneath him and three more hanging above him, illustrating that he has endured great suffering that has now finally ended—a child and a woman behind the tomb, welcoming their knight. The Four of Swords symbolizes a calm state of mind and rest after a significant event in your life - good or bad.

Five of Swords

The card illustrates a man looking with contempt at the masses he has conquered. He has five swords - all of which he has gained from his enemies. Two figures walk away, showing their dissatisfaction with the outcome, further underlined by the clouds gathering in the sky. The Five of Swords indicates that your recent success may be going against the interest of others.

Six of Swords

This card paints an image of a woman and a child in a boat heading to land. Their backs are facing you, but it's evident that they are leaving something behind from their position. The boat and the six swords represent their strength to move towards a more promising future. The Six of Swords reminds you that you need to move on, regardless of the loss you are experiencing.

Seven of Swords

On this card, a man is sneaking away from a camp and carrying five swords in his hands, leaving two other swords on the ground behind him. Also, behind him, a group of soldiers is raising the alarm on discovering he has escaped. The Seven of Swords shows that even when your actions are sneaky, and you think that you are getting away with them, sooner or later, you will have to face the consequences.

Eight of Swords

You see a woman tied up on this card, with eight swords trapping her in place. Because she is also blindfolded, she can't see the gaps between the swords through which she could escape. The barren land and the gray sky behind her indicate that she can't see any hope of breaking free. The Eight of Swords points out that if you allow a foreign entity to seize control over your life, you give away your power to make changes.

Nine of Swords

This card depicts a woman sitting on her bed, holding her head in her hands as if she were just awakened from a nightmare. Above the woman are nine swords and a carving of a person being defeated below her, which alludes to the cause of the nightmares. The Nine of Swords shows that grief can be a heavy burden to carry alone, and you sometimes need to find someone with whom you can share it.

Ten of Swords

This card shows a man lying face down on the ground, a red cloth covering his entire body, and ten swords stabbed into his back. The black sky above him and the eerily calm weather illustrate the negative emotions associated with his death. The Ten of Swords indicates a low point in your life – possibly the result of the misuse of power.

Page of Swords

This card presents a young person standing on rocky ground, with the wind blowing their hair and the trees behind him. With a determined and challenging expression on his face and a sword in his hand, this young person is ready to act at any minute. The Page of Swords illustrates that you are a great communicator, full of new ideas, and always ready for a passionate debate.

Knight of Swords

This card shows a young man wearing armor, sitting on a horse in the middle of a battle. The cape of the knight and the horse's harness are decorated with birds and butterflies. Behind them, there are stormy clouds, and trees are tossed around by the wind. The horse's white color symbolizes the energy the knight possesses to overcome any challenge. The Knight of Swords shows that strong goals will help you overcome the obstacles in front of you.

Queen of Swords

This card depicts a woman, the queen, wearing a grim look and staring into the distance while seated on a throne in the clouds. She has a sword in her right hand, pointing it towards the sky, whereas her left hand is extended in a gesture of offering. The Queen of Cards highlights the importance of reflecting on your situation instead of making decisions based on emotions.

King of Swords

This card shows a king holding a double-edged sword while sitting on his throne. He is pointing it upwards, highlighting his intellect, power, and authority in all things. His blue tunic symbolizes spiritual enlightenment, while the butterflies on the throne indicate transformation. The King of Swords rules over all the logical systems on earth and carries powerful messages about the possible outcome of your actions.

Pentacles

The suit of Pentacles is associated with the Hebrew letter ה (He), the earth element and Assiah, the World of Manifestation, and the Faculty of Bodily Sensations.

Ace of Pentacles

This card depicts a hand emerging from the clouds holding a gold coin engraved with a pentagram. Below the hand, a lush garden made up of fertile lands is watered by the creek of emotions running nearby. Behind it, a mountain rises, displaying the ambition required when searching for the pentacle. The Ace of Pentacles illustrates that if you want good results from your ideas, you must put in the effort to cultivate them.

Two of Pentacles

This card depicts a man dancing in choppy waters and juggling two coins. The coins are surrounded by the infinity sign, which implies that he will handle all the issues that come his way gracefully. In the background, two ships are struggling to float on the huge waves, proving how balanced the man's act is. The Two of Pentacles represents the ups and downs of everyday life.

Three of Pentacles

This card displays a young apprentice discussing his progress in building a cathedral with a priest and a nobleman. Despite his lack of experience, the ideas of the apprentice are captivating enough for the other two to listen to him. The Three of Pentacles shows that all projects require a variety of expertise. If you want to finish them, you will need to work with people possessing different skills from your own.

Four of Pentacles

This card illustrates a man sitting on a stool, rigorously guarding his pentacles. One of them seems to be on his head, another one is clutched between his hands, and two pentacles are underneath his feet. The Four of Pentacles indicates that obsessing over maintaining your wealth will turn you into its captive. You will become a possessive and greedy person unable to feel or do anything else.

Five of Pentacles

The card shows two figures walking outside in the snow, looking cold, tired, and possibly ill. One of them is on crutches, while the other has a shawl on their head but no shoes. Behind them, there is a black wall with five pentacles in the window, suggesting it's a sanctuary. The Five of Pentacles conveys the loss of an important item, financial adversities, or personal casualty.

Six of Pentacles

This card paints an image of a man dressed in purple robes, symbolizing his status and wealth. With one hand, he balances a scale, showing he treats everyone equally. With his other hand, he is handing out coins to beggars who are kneeling in front of him. The Six of Pentacles emphasizes the importance of charity, regardless of the size of your wealth.

Seven of Pentacles

The card shows a man resting on a shovel and taking a break from his labor to enjoy the garden he is making. But because it's not finished, he cannot touch the fruit yet. There are seven pentacles hanging from the plants, but he will keep only one of them. The Seven of Pentacles reassures you of your larger goals, encouraging you not to focus on short-term results, but work for the ultimate reward.

Eight of Pentacles

This card depicts a man engraving a pentacle symbol into the eight golden coins. There is a town in the background, but he is so absorbed in his work that he is completely unaware of any distractions. The Eight of Pentacles urges you to prioritize your projects and address them in order of urgency. This way, you will always be able to deliver the best version of your work and won't be distracted by the variety of tasks.

Nine of Pentacles

On this card, you can see a woman in a vineyard. The vines are rich in grapes and golden coins, indicating successful ventures and material wealth. She is wearing a long dress adorned with sunflowers and playing with a falcon sitting in her hand. The Nine of Pentacles conveys all the security and reassurance optimal financial wealth can bring you.

Ten of Pentacles

On this card, an older man rests in an archway and is surrounded by younger people. His robe is adorned with moon crescents and vines, representing the spiritual and material world. In front of him, a happy couple and a small child is playing with a dog, all of which indicate his true legacy. The Ten of Pentacles shows that whatever you create will become part of a legacy that will stand for a long time.

Page of Pentacles

The card illustrates a young man walking in a field of flowers. Behind him, there are several lush trees, but he doesn't notice anything as he is so enthralled by the coin in his hand and all the things it represents. The Page of Pentacles signals that you are too absorbed in your ambition and diligence to obtain financial security that you become unaware of all the blessings nature can give you.

Knight of Pentacles

The card shows a knight sitting on a dark horse in a field, where he is preparing for the harvest. Unlike the other knight, he does not fight, believing he can do more on the field. He has a gold coin in his hand, considering how to get the most out of it. The Knight of the Pentacles brings on concerns about long-term goals and your responsibility to all you have given duties.

Queen of Pentacles

This card shows a beautiful queen sitting on a throne decorated with various elements of the earth, referring to her close ties with nature. The coin in her hand symbolizes prosperity, but the rabbit springing into the frame on the right-hand side of the card points to caution. The Queen of Pentacles warns you if you are about to leap in the wrong direction while chasing success.

King of Pentacles

This card illustrates a king sitting on a throne that is adorned with vines and carvings of bulls. He is also surrounded by vines and flowers, showing he is attached to his wealth. He has a coin with a pentacle engraved on it in his left hand and a scepter in his right hand, which shows his protectiveness. The King of Pentacles encourages growth – both on a financial plane and a personal one.

Chapter 7: Kabbalistic Astrology

Kabbalah is a Jewish tradition that explains humanity's wisdom behind and essence. According to popular folklore, when Prophet Adam was expelled from Eden, he received a book from Archangel Raziel that contained secrets of this universe and was intended to help Adam adapt to his surroundings. This mysterious knowledge was passed down through generations, from biblical prophets in ancient history like Melchizedek (the priest-king), Abraham, Isaac, and Jacob.

With the dispersion of Jews throughout Europe, their teachings and this ancient knowledge were transmitted secretly and at great risk. Ironically enough, some Jewish scholars prohibited astrology for eons, and Rabbis strictly abstained from astrology, particularly during the medieval era. This conflict of reason and faith persists even in today's Modern era. Simply put, followers of Kabbalistic astrology believe it sheds light on the level of consciousness you happen to be at the moment.

As Above, So Below

The sole purpose of Kabbalistic astrology is to be free from the influence of the cosmos and resume control of your life. According to the Kabbalah's mythology, the universe was created by God to act as an image of his divine self. Kabbalists work toward perfecting both visible and invisible worlds to serve God. This is contrary to the misconceptions about Kabbalah that merely link it with magical rituals.

The principle of "as above, so below" dictates that the position of the heavenly bodies influences the physical world. The reverse of this concept is also true, "as below, so above," and according to this reversed version, our actions carry far more impact than we may realize. Whatever we do in the physical world can contribute to discord or harmony in the world higher up in the heavens. This sheds light on the very makeup of the matrix of the universe, wherever the physical and spiritual are deeply intertwined.

Planetary Alignment and Tree of Life

The Tree of Life holds a central symbolic position in the Kabbalistic ideology and facilitates explanations of universal principles. It is a diagram consisting of 10 circles, known as "Sefirot," and each of these Sefirot symbolically represents an aspect of God which is, in turn, inter-linked by 22 different paths. It is believed that at the time of the conception of this Universe, God essentially withdrew from existence toward the resulting void and entered the 10 Sefirot, and that was how they came to hold the ten aspects of God (this process is called Tzimtsum or contraction).

On the diagram, there is a non-Sefirah as well, also called Da'at, which signifies a place of knowledge and is a portal of sorts offering access to different worlds. The Tree of Life has Sefirots arranged in three columns. The right column symbolizes "energy," the left one represents "form," and the middle column denotes "consciousness." Since this diagram is thought to be representative of the entire makeup and mysteries of the universe, it applies to all the different situations that we may ever encounter (including through the use of astrology). From an astrological perspective, all the planets (including earth) can be placed within the Sefirot.

These 10 Sefirot correspond to the 10 Holy Commandments, and each has its own angel linked to them. In Kabbalistic Astrology, the birth chart is mapped in the form of the Tree of Life and reflects a clear astrological mapping of the solar system with the position of stars and planets. Besides, as we mentioned earlier, the Tree of Life demonstrates the soul's journey from past to present and its purpose on earth.

The Tree of Life provides a map of the consciousness and the body. Therefore, it is vital to review the Sefirot name, its related body area, planetary association, and important qualities.

The top of the body is known as "Keter," the skull or crown. It includes Chochmah, which represents the right brain and holds the qualities of Uranus, which means it has very bright inspiration. "Binah" is the second Sefirah, which represents the left brain, has Saturn-like qualities and holds onto boundary, form, and container. The last in the category of "body" or Keter is "Da'at" or central brain (knowledge), which is associated with the unknowable one or the mysterious one.

The next category is of arms that include "Chesed," which is also known as the right arm or kindness, and relates to Nepture and Jupiter with attributes of expansion and boundlessness. This category also has Gevurah, known as left arm or severity, with attributes similar to planet Mars and having focus, action, and direction.

The torso is defined by Tiferet (heart and beauty), linked with self-centered awareness, sun, and radiance.

The category of legs includes Netzach (kidney, victory, or right leg) and is associated with the planet Venus showing qualities of loving self-esteem. This category also holds "Hod" (left leg, kidney, and glory), which relates to the planet Mercury and is dominated by the attribute of orderliness and logical thinking.

The last two are Yesod which form the foundational point and which represents sexual organs. Yesod is also linked with the magnetic attraction of the Moon. While Malkuth (mouth, feet, or Kingship) is a symbol for the earth and embodies everything that is on the earthly plane, its supports are defined and are a firm foundation.

The 22 Hebrew letters serve as pathways that connect different Sefirot. You can use each letter to help with meditation or take a combination of letters depending on what you want to achieve in your meditation.

Jacob's Ladder

There have been various books written about Kabbalah that refer to the astrological side of the belief system, but one book written by Z'ev ben Shimon Halevi stands out in particular. The book contains details of Kabbalistic astrology and extensive descriptions. Moreover, the charting of the Tree of Life also evolved during medieval Spain, and although modern Kabbalists were comfortable with the Sefirot and planetary correspondence, Halevi highlighted Jacob's ladder on the extended Tree of Life. For this reason, Halevi is also crowned as a principal practitioner of the Toledo Tradition that was practiced in Spain, where Kabbalah gained popularity during the 14th and 15th centuries.

The four worlds in Jacob's Ladder, Azilut (Divine), Beriah (spirit of Creation), Yetzirah (forms), and Assiyah (Physical), show an overlap with one another. Also, on Jacob's Ladder, the planetary system has been placed upon Yetzirah (the second-lowest level). It is also labeled as the world corresponding to the human psyche and is the focus of astrological studies.

Mother Letters in Kabbalistic Astrology

The Tree of Life can be explored in several ways. One way is to recognize the energies in the three Mother Letters: Aleph, Mem, and Shin. The mother letters are symbolized by the horizontal branches of the Tree of Life, while the seven visible planets are symbolized by the vertical branches.

'Aleph' is the first mother letter and resides in the body, across the heart-space. There are no particular sounds associated with it.

As it is the first letter, it is used as a method to begin action. "Aleph" urges you to pay attention and become more aware of your heart space and ribcage. To do so, you can start by taking three deep breaths and making the "Aleph" sounds while exhaling. This letter is linked with the element of air and has a creative spark associated with it. It is also a balancing point between the elements of water and fire.

The letter mem is found between hips in the pelvic region, and it is also the letter at the beginning of the Hebrew word for water, linking it to the sea of consciousness. It is also connected with the Hebrew word "maggid," which translates to angel and sheds light on the connection to your guide and teachers. While practicing breathing, make the MMMM sound and pay attention to the pelvic and hip regions. This letter supports a deeper connection with the emotional body and is associated with the element of water.

The third mother letter is "Shin," which resides between the left and right brain. The words "shalom" (peace), "Shabbat" (rest), and "shanna" (the year with wholeness) begin with the letter "Shin." This letter is linked to the element of fire and is used for transformative and integrative purposes. When wanting to meditate while integrating several perspectives, it is a great tool

Placement of Mars and Venus

It is interesting to examine the planetary alignment on the Tree of Life because various unexpected or anomalous points emerge. If you have previous knowledge of astrology, you may be surprised that Mars is found on the passive column of the Tree at Gevurah, as it is known as the planet of assertion. In comparison, Venus is famous as a harmonious and loving planet and is found on the active site of the Tree at Netzach.

The explanations for these placements make perfect sense and offer in-depth insight into the very core of astrological science. The analogy of a martial artist whose mode of attack is "non-movement" and only strikes at the right moment can be taken. This type of discipline of judgment precision is a defining attribute of Gevurah. Similarly, the Netzach Sefirah that corresponds to the planet Venus symbolically represents a young girl to denote the principle of attraction. As per her typical nature, this young lady (Venus) is anything but passive because she would make suggestive gestures to attract her mate.

Concept of Growth and Destruction

To an astrologer with a more traditional perspective, the Kabbalistic placement is intuitive because of the arrangement of the synchronized planets. For instance, the right pillar of the Tree emphasizes growth and has beneficent planets, like Jupiter and Venus, while the left pillar of the Tree of Life represents the depth and destructive passions and contains maleficent planets, like Saturn and Mars.

On the active pillar of the Tree, which symbolizes growth, we find Venus (moist and cool) and Jupiter (moist and warm). This is because the attribute of "moistness" is mainly associated with growth and fertilization. Conversely, on the pillar representing destruction, we find Saturn (cold and dry) and Mars (hot and dry) because both planets are dry in nature, and nothing grows in a dry environment (devoid of water). But when you ponder over the great logic behind this pillar placement and chart, it becomes clear that both the columns (growth and destruction) are essential for maintaining existence. So, the planets on the destructive r plane should not be shunned. Instead, they are welcomed, embraced, and celebrated similarly to the planets focusing on growth. The destructive planets are essential because they, in a way, pave the way for the new. It is quite similar to the concept of Yin-Yang, where the light portion contains a dot of darkness and the dark one has a dot of light.

According to the philosophy behind the Tree of Life, when existence gets too monotonous or unadventurous, some kind of action automatically brings back the lost state of equilibrium. Similarly, an excess of action can also initiate fragmentation of the universe, so to maintain equilibrium, a contraction or halt must be triggered in similar situations.

In a nutshell, this philosophy dictates that one state will trigger the other state in an attempt to restore balance, which is true in our daily lives because we do not seek to be excessively passive or active. We strive to hold onto a balanced amount of the qualities from both sides of the Tree of Life.

Mercury's Placement

Mercury is placed on the left pillar of the Tree at Hod, which represents "reverberation," as it has a changeable nature. Similar to Saturn and Mars, Mercury has a dry nature. However, Mercury has a reputation as the juggler that throws balls in the air without actually moving ahead as it tends to pick up on the attributes of any planet near it, which is why mercury represents "form" better than energy and is placed in the passive pillar of the tree of life.

The Sun and Moon Positions

While studying Kabbalistic astrology, you will notice one key difference from all conventional astrological sciences: they use different calendars. According to conventional astrology, you would use either the Gregorian or the Solar calendar. In contrast, Kabbalistic astrology uses the Hebrew calendar and considers the positions of the moon and the sun. This enables us to take control of the astrological influences each month.

The Sun and Moon are representative of self-consciousness and ego consciousness, respectively. They also symbolize the world and those who are unique and act according to their thoughts in particular, and those who tend to follow mass opinions. The path of honesty is the path between these two. When analyzing the relationship between the Sun and Moon according to this perspective, it adds another layer of meaning to the natal chart. The Moon, located at Yesod, represents our everyday world and the way we react to different situations, while the zodiac placement of the Sun represents our decisions from a higher perspective.

The placement of Moon at the Yesod position is good because it is important to deal with it in our everyday life; being egotistical in daily life situations is not helpful. It creates chaos when our ego tries to interfere with the position of the Sun as a ruler, and our ego later becomes invaluable. Therefore, when someone is behaving differently than their sun sign, it is because they regard the Moon as their ruler.

Kabbalistic Astrology and Tarot

In general and very broad terms, Kabbalistic Astrology and Tarot both come under the esoteric category because of their inherently mystical nature. The Tree of Life in Kabbalah is one central theme that unifies the Kabbalistic Astrology and Tarot card decks in Kabbalistic ideology.

According to conventional astrology, the birth chart gives a detailed map of an individual's life and how the planets affect them. However, Kabbalistic maps out an individual's consciousness in the context of the cosmos around us. There are 22 letters in the Hebrew alphabet and 22 cards in the Major Arcana in a Tarot deck. We have discussed how closely Tarot cards and Kabbalah have been linked through centuries. These 22 letters are further divided into three exclusive categories:

- Three mother letters relate to Air, Fire, and Water elements. In this sequence, you will notice that "earth" is not included, even though it seems to be an important theme here. In reality, the element of "earth" is ever-present because it embodies and exists in everything.

- The seven double letters are associated with the visible planets.

- Twelve letters that connect to Zodiac symbols or months of the year.

According to the Kabbalistic Astrology, four universes relate to the four realms of life and the four elements:

- The spiritual plane and the divine world ('Atzilut') are associated with the element of "fire." The mental plane and intellectual world ('Beriah') are associated with the element of "air."

- The emotional plane and the psychological world ('Yetzirah') with the element of "water."

- The physical plane and the material world are associated with the element of "earth."

Healing of Immanence

In Kabbalistic astrology, the healer can envision and focus on the base of the Tree of Life, which is the earth element. Often, it is described as "the earth lacking light of its own and having a space of gravity, center, and awareness." The Kabbalistic healer tries to embody a place of consciousness by remembering that the Divine presence takes over everything while conducting a healing session. In fact, there is no place the G-d is not present, so there is nowhere to go. This is the core teaching of Kabbalah that the Divine encompasses every aspect of creations, and they are essentially a manifestation of the Divine God.

Initially, the concepts under Kabbalistic Astrology, including the Tree of Life, Jacob's ladder, and the corresponding planetary alignment, may appear to be overly complex. But when you study them, they are quite simple and carry a unique perspective to understand the mysteries of this universe.

Chapter 8: Spreads and Conducting Readings

Now that you have familiarized yourself with the general meaning of the Major Arcana and Minor Arcana cards and their relation to the Kabbalistic Astrology, you are ready to start experimenting with tarot readings yourself. After all, there's no better way to see how tarot spreads can reveal the answers to your questions than by inquiring. However, we want to emphasize that reading the tarot is not a form of advice or prediction.

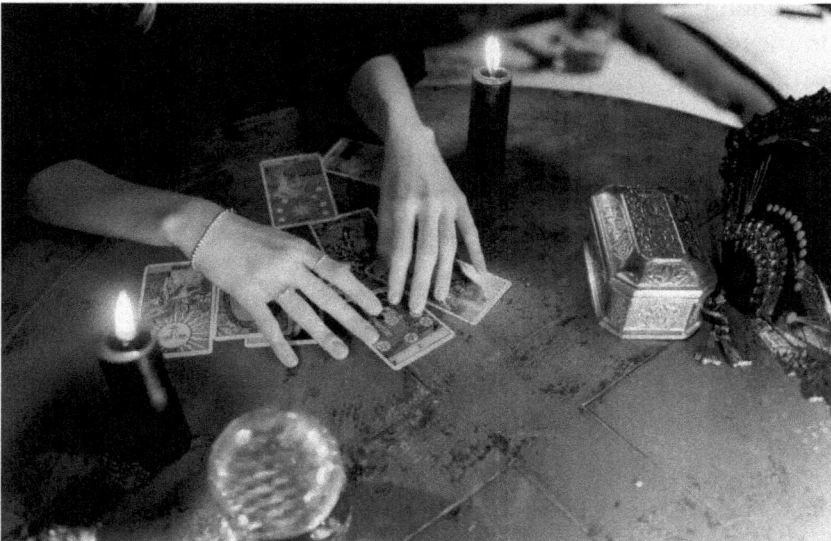

The cards can only reveal possible outcomes based on your current actions, but these outcomes should never be interpreted as a given or be accepted as factual. One must be responsible for their own life and choices and use the spreads only as a tool to reveal innermost desires. Remember, tarot – and Kabbalistic tarot- works with spiritual energy. This means that the outcomes revealed by the cards can change just as quickly as your energy does. This chapter contains examples of a few simple spreads – and in which you can learn and practice how to transfer your energy to the cards and interpret their meaning. Lastly, you will gain an insight into the Kabbalistic Tree of Life tarot, an intrinsic spread tied to all the realms.

One-Card Spread

The best way to get to know your deck is to start with a one-card spread. Whether you want to pull and contemplate one card during your daily Kabbalistic meditation or journal about the individual cards, or you can pull a card whenever you need a question answered at any time throughout the day. While this process takes a bit longer, you will benefit from it in the long run. Concentrating on one card at a time will allow you to memorize its meaning, symbolism, and nuance. It helps you sense each card's complex energy and connect to this energy with your own. Once you see how their energy relates to yours, you will learn to recognize the themes and messages they are sending.

Before you start the reading, it's always good to determine your reason for consulting the cards. Start by focusing your mind on your intention. Meditation, a quick energy scan, or a short breathing exercise can help you tune into your body and mind. Make sure you formulate your question ahead of time so that you won't get confused during the reading. With a one-card spread, it's best to focus on one or eventually two questions the most with each card. Writing the intent on a piece of paper will help you to memorize it.

Here are some simple but insightful questions to ask during the one-card spread:

- What do I need to learn today?
- What message is my intuition sending to me?

- Which card can help me this day, week, month, or year?
- Which card will get me into alignment today?
- What can help me on my healing journey?
- How can I be of assistance today?
- Which of my strengths will I need today?
- Where do I need more acceptance and love?
- What can I express or share with others?

If you require the help of a spiritual guide during the reading, now is the time to call on them as well. Kabbalistic tarot suggests relying on your highest self – but you are free to use whatever guide you feel will be the most helpful in each situation. If it's your first time using a deck, or you haven't used it in a while, you should also cleanse your deck from malicious energy – with a purifying incense, candle, or spell (earlier chapters in this book have given you an idea of how to do this).

Having done that, you can now move on to posing your questions and choosing a card. Place the paper with your question in front of you and repeat it in your mind while you are shuffling the deck. Once you feel the need to stop, pick a card and turn it over. You can pull a card from any part of the deck – as long as it feels right to you.

Lay the card you've pulled on a flat surface and reflect on its message. This will probably be the hardest part of the exercise as you might not feel the connection to the card. This is normal, and you may even be tempted to look for another card. However, you must remember that the card has come to you for a reason. You should trust that it knows what you need, even if its meaning doesn't make sense to you at the time. This is where journaling or meditation can come in handy. Through these exercises, you can explore a personal connection with the card you have pulled.

Feel free to research the meaning of the cards if you want to, but, in the end, the answers that lie in them are always related to your intent and what a specific card can tell you during a reading. Most importantly, it's your energy the cards are connected with, so their message will be the reflection of your inner voice. Look at the image on the card and focus on whatever comes to mind first, without second-guessing your thoughts. Only if nothing comes to mind should you refer to the general meaning of the cards before interpreting them.

Three-Card Spread

Consulting a three-card spread is helpful when you are still at the beginning of your Tarot journey, but you require a little more insight than a one-card pull can provide for you. Even if you are already familiar with the process, making a complex inquiry from three cards will always be quicker than consulting a more elaborate spread. This spread is one of the simplest ways to read multiple cards and tie their meaning into a story. From this story, you can get all the information you need, regardless of your experience or the problem you are having at the time.

As with the one-card spread, you start by setting your intent and writing down your questions. You can ask similar questions, too, except now you can ask more of them to figure out the entire story. Prepare yourself mentally and physically, and when you are ready, start shuffling your deck. Focusing on your intent, pull out three cards to which you are drawn. Lay them out in front of you, face-up, and examine them carefully, one by one. As you study the images on the cards before you, pay attention to how they make you feel. Make sure you notice the type of the cards well, as this will give you a clue about their relation to each other. For example, if the cards all belong to Major Arcana, their story holds a more substantial impact on your life.

The three cards tell a story, with a beginning, middle, and end – and this is exactly how you should view them. Think about the first card telling you about something that happened, the second revealing the event's outcome, and the third your reaction to it. Or, you can consider the cards as representing your past, present, and future life and consider the messages each of them is sending.

Having identified the individual meanings of the cards, now you must find the thread of the story that ties all three together. Sometimes, the narrative will be visible right away, while other times, you will need to ponder on it a bit more. Tap into your intuition – as this is where the story comes from. It may be a past event that affects your current or future life, a significant relationship, or an emotion that ties the cards together. Focus on what narrative feels right and trust it. Even if you can't understand the story yet, this will all make sense with time. Stay positive and don't force the process, no matter how frustrated you feel when learning to interpret your stories.

Practicing with this spread will make it easier to find what the cards have in common, how they relate to your intuition, and how to put them into perspective. It's a good idea to record your stories in a journal, particularly when you are still learning the ropes of tarot reading. You can always revisit them later and contemplate their meaning again to see if they make more sense. You will often find a feeling you have missed at the initial reading, and this may turn out to be the missing piece that ties everything together.

The Celtic Cross Spread

As a ten-card tarot spread, the Celtic Cross is more flexible and answers a more extensive range of questions than the previous two. What makes this spread great for newbies and professionals alike is that you can practice reading whether you have a specific question to ask or not. You can use it to examine different aspects of your life or simply assess a situation or event that took place in it. Still, creating a narrative from 10 cards is a lot more complicated than reading from one or three cards. For this reason, it's worth taking the time to explore the Celtic Cross spread and identify the positions of the cards in the specific formations. It will make it much easier to tie them together.

The preparation for reading a Celtic Cross spread is just as straightforward as it was with the previous two. The steps included are focusing your mind, setting your intent, formulating your questions, and starting to pull out the cards you feel drawn to. However, this is when things get a little more complicated. When you pick the first card, lay it down face up, in a vertical position, then place the second card on top of it – this type putting it horizontally. Place the third and the fourth cards beside the first one, left and right, respectively, in the same position. Put the fifth card above the first and the next one under it, in the same vertical position. You have now completed the first section of this spread – The Cross. Place the remaining four cards beside the cross, starting from the bottom and forming a straight horizontal line. This will be the second section called The Staff.

The six cards of the Cross-section provide a full picture of all that's occurring in your life – whether they cause changes within you or in outside circumstances affecting you. To analyze the full impact on your event, you must examine the Staff section. It will show you how the context affects each situation and exert your influence over it. The cards of the Cross can be broken down in several ways. Within it, you can observe the central circle consisting of two cards and reveal your answer's main part. Around that circle, there are four cards representing the events or areas of life the answer relates to.

Moving one step further, you can split the Cross into two different sections. The first ones are horizontal cards symbolizing time, whereas the vertical cards represent your consciousness. Therefore, reading both vertical and horizontal spreads paint a picture of two smaller spreads, revealing your conscious and unconscious desires and your past, present, and future.

Now, you are ready to focus on the individual position of the cards, which can reveal:

1. **Your Present or Inner Self:** This card allows you to see what's happening in your life in the present time or reveal the current state of your mind.

2. **The Problem:** Representing the challenge you are facing in the present time; the card shows you what you need to resolve to make progress forward.

3. **Your Past:** Observing the past event through this card shows how these events have shaped the current situation.

4. **Your Future:** This card represents possible outcomes that may come to be true given that nothing in your current thoughts, emotions, and actions changes. They won't provide a final resolution to your problems.

5. **Your Conscious Mind:** This card helps explore what your mind is focused on. Typically, it will reveal your goals, desires, and assumptions regarding the situation you are focused on.

6. **Your Subconscious:** The card of your subconscious reveals the driving force behind this situation, including the beliefs, thoughts, and feelings you may not understand yet.

7. **Your Influence:** In general, this card relates to how you see yourself and how this can influence the outcome of your current situation. The beliefs you carry, your ability to limit yourself or grow personally, all these factors are under your influence.

8. **External Factors:** This card depicts how the elements of the world around you affect your current situation. Apart from your emotional and social environment, it also highlights how others perceive you.

9. **Your Hopes and Fears:** This card highlights the paradoxical nature of people – representing both what you desire and what you are trying to avoid – even if they are the same exact thing.

10. **The Outcome:** As a summary of all the previous messages, this card predicts a likely resolution to the current or future events, given all that is happening in and around you.

Remember that the last card will not always show the outcome you desire. In this case, you have two different courses to take. You can either analyze the rest of the cards in hopes of finding a clue about a different outcome or file the reading away and revisit it a bit later to see if the resolution seems more favorable than it initially did.

Kabbalistic Tree of Life Spread

Drawing inspiration from the sephirot of the Kabbalistic Tree of Life, this spread is an excellent tool for revealing the relationships between all things in the universe. It permeates four dimensions: spiritual, psychological, emotional, and physical, and can be used with Jewish mandalas, such as Shiviti. The ten nodes on this tree represent the mysteries of each one of the realms, and they will provide an insight into your deeply hidden thoughts and desires. More importantly, this spread can be used to understand how the events in each of the realms affect your life and use this information to set up significant goals. This spread is challenging and is only recommended to attempt after you have mastered the simpler ones.

Once again, the preparation is the same as it is for all tarot readings, divination, or spiritual practices. Before starting to draw your cards, you must clear your mind, which, with this spread, is best done through meditation. This exercise allows for more extensive preparation – something that will benefit you greatly when the time comes to interpret and connect the cards.

When you feel ready, start drawing your cards and placing them face down before you, starting with the first one in the upper part of your surface. Place the second one to its right and the third one to its left. Then, put the fourth card under the second card and the fifth under the third. The seventh goes under the fourth and the eighth under the firth. The sixth card should be placed between the previous four and the first one. The night goes under the sixth, while the tenth is placed under the ninth. Now, you should have a trunk consisting of cards 6,9,10, two branches formed by cards 3, 5, 8, and 2, 4, 7, respectively, and card number 1 connecting the two branches.

While the deeper spiritual meaning of each card plays a more determining role in your reading, you can use the following interpretation based on the position of the cards:

1. **The Problem:** This card represents the highest ideal or goal you want to attain through active energy. However, this is only the first facet of the underlying issue.

2. **The Cause:** The card highlights the second aspect of the underlying issue – the driving force behind your problem. It can also represent a physical manifestation of the problem, such as a person.

3. **A New Power:** This card illustrates newly formed forces that will either aid or hinder you in life. It may refer to acute influences or oppositions.

4. **An Old Power:** Another card that shows forces that can act for you and against you. This time they are older and stand for objects and relationships you hold dear and sacred.

5. **Superficial Feelings:** This card represents the impact you will have on others while working toward your goal. It refers to the emotional state and the thoughts, fears, and desires you

invoke.

6. **Deep Emotions:** Referring to the same facet as the previous card position in this spread, this card represents your physical and mental health concerning how you affect others.

7. **The Physical World:** This card shows how your relationships, your own body and mind, your home environment, and your physical possession influence your life.

8. **Your Persona:** Representing an image outward, this card offers an insight into which goal you may find fulfilling based on how your project yourself and how others perceive you.

9. **The Advice:** This card unlocks your hidden potential by revealing your innermost passions. It often combines your heart's desires with your rationale, showing you the path ahead.

10. **The Wisdom:** The final card represents the wisdom you can find in your interaction with the physical world. Offering a takeaway, the card opens the potential for personal growth and allows you to learn everything you need to handle future issues.

While the goal of the Tree of Life Tarot reading is to access a source of greater wisdom through the cards, you should never focus on the individual cards. Remember, the Tree of Life doesn't consist solely of ten sefirot representing the ten realms. It also has 22 connecting paths between the sefirot, and these are just as vital as the realms themselves. Make sure you pay attention to how the individual cards relate to each other. Look at the paths they form as they connect to one another.

Another thing to keep in mind is the specific order in both laying out the cards and interpreting them. As you know, the Tree of Life roots are located at the base and move upward. They represent the highest of the realms, and the cards in their position are the most valuable in this tarot spread. Don't worry if this sounds a bit confusing at the beginning. With practice and insight, everything becomes clearer – which is why it's fundamental to master the basic tarot spreads before jumping into this one.

Chapter 9: Divination and Scrying Techniques

In the previous chapter, you have read about Tarot readings – which are great for a quick consult on daily issues. But what if you need information about a broader subject that may affect your future or find out if you are making the right decisions when working towards your goals? In this case, you must turn toward different divination forms employing the power of the Tarot and Kabbalah.

While this may sound like Tarot cards can predict the future, this is certainly not the case. They can help you figure out yours by offering you a guideline and a glimpse of where you are headed on your current course of life. Tarot cards and even Kabbalistic symbols can convey a message, but it will be up to you to decipher it. The way you interpret these messages and the actions you decide to take on receiving them will determine your fate and not the divination session itself. You are the largest co-creator of your destiny; you are just getting a little assistance from whatever divination tool you are using.

Another thing to keep in mind is just as the cards show what you need during simple reading, they will also guide you towards the future you truly desire. By connecting to your inner wisdom, they unveil hidden desires and help you understand them better. More often than not, the results of your divination session will surprise you.

Simple Divination Techniques

There are many ways to use Tarot and Kabbalah in your divination practices and reveal details about your life cycle. Pick one card and maybe a few additional ones for clarification if necessary. Advanced practitioners would pull one card from several decks as, through experience and use, they have formed different energetic connections with each of them. This allows them to get more information on the subject they are looking into. However, for starters, you can use the simple methods described below.

One-Card Divination

A simple exercise like transferring your energy to the card you have chosen can reveal a specific story you need to experience to live a better life. For this, you will need to find a quiet spot, do a few deep breathing exercises so you can relax, and focus on the task ahead. When ready, shuffle your deck and pull out the first card you feel drawn to. Look at it briefly, then close your eyes and step into the card's imagery in your mind. This will enhance your visualization skills and psychic ability. Different cards hint at different trials and tribulations that may await you in the near future.

For example, the Major Arcana cards represent the energy of your guides. These are cards your ancestors, deities, and other spirits convey their messages through. They will most likely appear if you need general guidance in life. On the other hand, if you happen to pull a card from the Minor Arcana suits, you will be facing challenges related to people and specific situations. For instance, drawing the four of cups warns you to stop ignoring an emotion about an upcoming event.

You should focus on calling on whatever image comes to mind when holding a card. Pay attention to the thoughts, emotions, and sensory stimuli that immediately flood your mind when looking at a specific card. These are the products of your spiritual energy permeating them. When you have a clear image in mind, take a deep breath, open your eyes, and consider the message's meaning. If the card fails to produce an image you can associate with any part of your life, you may pull another one to see if that one helps you to understand the message.

Three-Card Divination

Similar to the previous one, a three-card spread can also be used for specific divination purposes. Namely, if you have a question that requires just a "yes" or "no" answer, you will need the reinforcement of the additional cards. Do this exercise in a space where you can focus your thoughts and spend as much time as you need to mull things over. Shuffle your deck, and when you are ready, pull out three cards from the deck at random. The top card (the first one) will be the most important one but make sure to pay attention to the other two.

For example, if you want to find out if you should consider a job offer you have just received, the top card will tell you whether it's a good idea. The other two cards will either reinforce the message of the first one or deny it. Even if the first one says go ahead and do it – the other two may warn you about potential issues with that specific offer. If they come in the reversed form, they will also evoke negative images in your mind.

This is a specific question that requires a concrete answer, so you must ascertain that the cards tell you about the event you are interested in. Make sure to take in the imagery of the top card to see if it really talks about that job offer and not about other events or influences. After visualizing and interpreting all three cards, take a little time to consider the good and the bad side of the situation before deciding.

If you aren't interested in knowing about events in your future but are happy to ignore specific details, you can use the time limitation version of this same technique. Here, you must decide on a course of action just before pulling the three cards and then ask them about the outcome that follows in the next three to six months. The further ahead you are trying to look, the more likely you will be to change your path, altering the possible outcome.

Using Crystal Grids

A crystal grid in the form of the Tree of Life can also be used to empower your divination skills. To make a powerful grid based on the question you ask of the Tree of Life, you will need to include crystals for psychic enhancement during the divination. While this symbol is mostly known for bringing balance into your life, sometimes, you can only achieve this after getting some of your questions answered. The most effective crystals for this purpose are amethyst, blue lace agate, citrine, labradorite, polychrome jasper, red jasper, and white agate.

But how do crystal grids work? It's quite simple. When you choose a geometric pattern and place the stones on it, you open a doorway for spiritual energy. The crystal grid absorbs this energy, transforms it into a form you can use the most, and directs it toward your manifestation. This can be either a place, an object, a concept, or a person if you are gridding for someone else. In a way, gridding works the same as prayers, journeying, reading, or any other divination technique. Remember, the answer you are seeking doesn't only come from your energy. Your higher self, your ancestors, and spiritual guides may also direct you. Crystal grids allow you to connect with their energy.

Now that you understand how they work, it's time for you to learn how to set up and use one. Start by clearing your space – this applies to both your mind and the area where you will be working. You can use incense, salts, or any other method, even physically cleaning the space if that works for you. Expel any unnecessary energy from your space, and start preparing yourself mentally. Draw or make a circle around the spot where you'll be grinding and sit down in its middle. The circle is there to mark the area where the energy will be directed from the entire space. Turn off your electronics, and if you are working outside, make sure to be away from similar distractions.

If you have a special surface you would like to use to create the grid, lay it on the ground. It's fine if you don't have anything special. Any flat surface will work – as long as the grid can remain safe during the ritual. Now, set your intention. Remember, the intention is energy flowing through time and space. Since it doesn't have a specific shape, it can't be contained for a long period. The crystal grid will help you focus on it long enough to manifest it – but for this to work, you will need to make it clear enough so the grid can catch it. While the Tree of Life is a powerful symbol, you may need another incentive to focus on. Whether it's a representation of your spiritual guide, or anything else, holding it in front of you will force your mind to concentrate on your goal. In fact, you can even use a deck of Tarot cards or just one card to serve you as an inspiration. This is particularly helpful if you cannot interpret the cards you have drawn in your previous Tarot readings.

When you feel you have an intention in mind, examine it to see if it's truly the concept you are going for. If you are sure it can help you get to the root of the issue, you will be ready to send your message to the universe through the grid. Using your intuition once again, select the crystal you will use. Make sure you feel a connection toward each one of them as they will be conducting your energy. You will also need a card with a Tree of Life pattern, which you will place in the center of the space. Start putting the crystals on it in a clockwise fashion. When you reach the top part of the pattern, move down towards the center pillar.

At this time, you may do an invocation or a prayer, further stabilizing your focus. Then, recite your intention out loud so the vibration of your voice can activate the transfer of energy through the crystals. Try to visualize what you are looking for in your future. Create an image of yourself in the situation you're interested to know more about and as many details as you can. Allow your body to feel what you are experiencing in your head.

Having activated the grid with your intention is only the start of the gridding process. You must channel the energy flow through your body to become one with the grid's energetic field. Start by touching one of the stones in the center of the symbol with your index finger. Next, trace the pattern from one stone to another, going through the same motion as you were when setting up the grid. Feel the energy flowing from the crystals as you connect the points of the grid.

When you establish a solid connection between the crystals and yourself, the grid will allow you to interact with it. You can state your message once again, loudly or in your mind, and send it to the universe. Feel free to take as much time as you need for this. If you feel you have finished, you can either close the grid or renew it. The latter option is great if you practice the gridding frequently and need your grid to stay up permanently. However, apart from considering it when setting up, you must maintain your grid too. The crystals should be cleansed after each gridding to prevent the residual energy from hindering the results of your next session. You can use the same method you used to cleanse your space.

Scrying

Scrying is another way to expand your divinatory skills. This practice involves projecting yourself into a reflective area and can use both the elements of the tarot and Kabbalah. There are several ways to scry, and you can apply any of your senses in the process. The most popular practices are visual scrying and audio scrying, with the first one being recommended for beginners.

Whichever method you opt for, your first step is to choose your medium. Water, dark sand, crystals, wax, fire, candle flame, tiles, and a black mirror are just some of the reflective surfaces that can serve as a medium. To incorporate scrying into your Kabbalistic practice, use a dark crystal sphere or a piece of glass or crystal-adorned with the Tree of Life.

Scrying may seem complicated and even intimidating, but with enough practice and dedication, anyone can master it. Make sure you start learning to scry in a place where you can work undisturbed. After developing your scrying skills, you will be able to do it anywhere you want to – as long as you have a medium to use.

Once you've determined your medium, find a quiet space – like you would for meditation. You can even dim your lights and make the room darker if it helps you focus. The key is to relax your mind, separate your thoughts about your everyday life and file them away so that they would bother you during scrying. Take a few deep breaths and let your worries dissipate until you feel your conscious being altered.

Set an intent for scrying. It can be anything from finding out what the future holds for you to asking for advice on a decision you need to make. It can even be your way of communicating with your higher self or another spiritual guide. Unlike Tarot readings, scrying works best with short descriptive sentences and not questions. So, try to describe what you are looking for as succinctly as possible and then focus on it. Write it down if it helps you bring it into the center of your conscious mind.

If you find formulating your intent anything other than a question challenging, at least do not make it an uncertain one. That said, asking yes or no questions when you are looking at one symbol won't help you either. Be demanding and get straight to the point by reciting something like this:

- What happens if I make this step?

- Show me the consequences of making this step.

- What can I expect from this particular situation?

- I want to know if this situation/event/ action will help me grow.

Gaze into the surface of your crystal and notice every detail about the Tree of Life symbol on it. Let your mind conjure up an image it associates with that symbol at that moment. Don't try to create new imagery even if you don't like what you see. In the beginning, the images may appear blurry, but the more you practice, the more vivid they will become. But even then, it may seem like a dream, which is entirely normal – just as it's typical to have a different experience at each scrying session. Sometimes, you will see simple shapes, and sometimes you will witness entire events like you would watching a movie. It all depends on your needs and connections with your medium and spiritual guides (if you are using any).

Whether you were going for visual scrying or not, your other senses can automatically be involved. If the message you need to retrieve is strong enough, you will probably hear, smell, taste, and feel things, even if you only want to see them. Another common occurrence during scrying is seeing/feeling dates and specific words. Make sure you write them down along with everything else you have experienced. They will often hold a clue for interpreting other parts of your message.

The process can take as long or as short a time as it needs to be for you to learn everything you want. When you feel you've experienced everything you need to, you can slowly let your thoughts come back automatically. If you are a beginner, you might find it hard to interpret the message right away. If this happens, leave it aside on the paper or journal you have written it down and return to it when you feel ready to decipher it. If you find scrying exhausting, feel free to take some time to ground yourself afterward. Eat, drink, rest in nature or do anything else you feel necessary to recharge your energy.

Whether you interpret the message right away or later, you should always let your intuition guide you. Even if your experience was negative, your intuition shows it to you for a reason. It may be related to an aspect of life you aren't aware of, or it can be a reflection of someone else's actions that are now affecting your life. If the experience changes when you scry, you are most likely receiving an alternate answer to your inquiry. To avoid confusion, go with the first one – as this one is coming from your gut. Most of the time, this is the correct one. Some messages will have a spiritual meaning, while others are more connected to your inner thoughts and feelings.

Conclusion

This book explores the interesting yet complex relationship between the Tarot and Kabbalah. It serves as a comprehensive guide that teaches you everything you need to know about Kabbalistic Tarot, divination, and astrology. Its easy-to-read-and-grasp structure makes it perfect for beginners, and its thoroughness makes it perfect for more experienced readers who wish to brush up on their knowledge. This book will be your ultimate go-to source whenever you need to double-check certain details.

Originating in northern Italy in the 14th and 15th centuries, with its figures and illustrations inspired by carnival parades, the Tarot deck remains among the most prominent divination tools today. The Tarot cards are the archetypal symbols that serve as a symbolic journey of the soul. Each card also leads to a path on the Kabbalistic Tree of Life, where the two belief systems connect.

The Kabbalistic tradition is a very ample source of Jewish mysticism and its practices. It provides a deep insight into its rituals and prayers. The majority of these practices are associated with exploring ways in which one can achieve oneness with the creator. However, the smaller portion of these rituals and prayers is directly or indirectly related to the Tarot. Most mystics precede their Kabbalistic practices with mindfulness techniques. These exercises range from basic breathing methods to more complex forms of meditation and yoga. They even often incorporate these exercises into the rituals themselves.

The Tree of Life uniquely depicts how the Creator expresses their creative energy by manifesting it into the universe. This can be seen through the existence of humans and more divine creatures like angels. The tree branches are symbols of essential creative sources that are overseen by a certain archangel. Those who practice Kabbalah suggest that you can forge a deeper spiritual connection with the divine if you focus on one of these energies.

The Fool's Journey is Major Arcana's collective path, according to Kabbalah. This journey illustrates one's descent into the physical world and their journey toward the light. At first, the Fool is presented as a raw form of energy. Then, the archetype walks the entire path of the Major Arcana until the traveler reaches their full potential. To evolve spirituality and become the best version of yourself, you have to follow the channels from one Sephira to the next. The Minor Arcana cards are more relevant to the physical realm and the world around us. They allow us to see the practical aspects of the physical and material world. This is why it's easier to get attuned with the Minor Arcana cards in our personal and professional lives.

The Kabbalistic system of astrology works within the framework of the Tree of Life, which is considered a map of the entire universe, with each sephira corresponding to a certain planet. This concept is associated with and can be applied to the Tarot. Tarot cards can be used for various purposes besides conducting readings. You can use them in other methods of divination and scrying and combine them with other tools to improve your psychic abilities.

Here's another book by Mari Silva that you might like

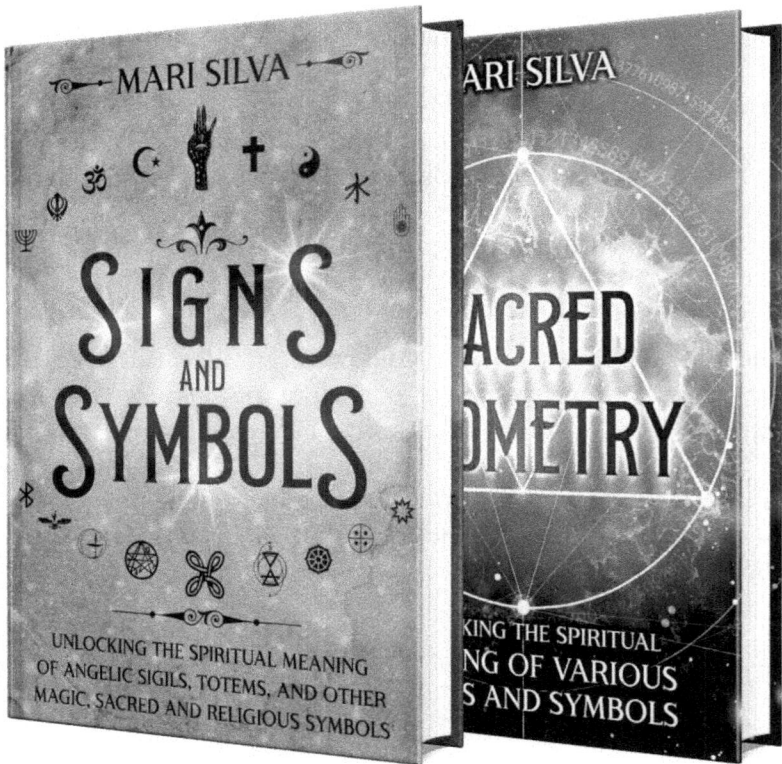

Your Free Gift
(only available for a limited time)

Thanks for getting this book! If you want to learn more about various spirituality topics, then join Mari Silva's community and get a free guided meditation MP3 for awakening your third eye. This guided meditation mp3 is designed to open and strengthen ones third eye so you can experience a higher state of consciousness. Simply visit the link below the image to get started.

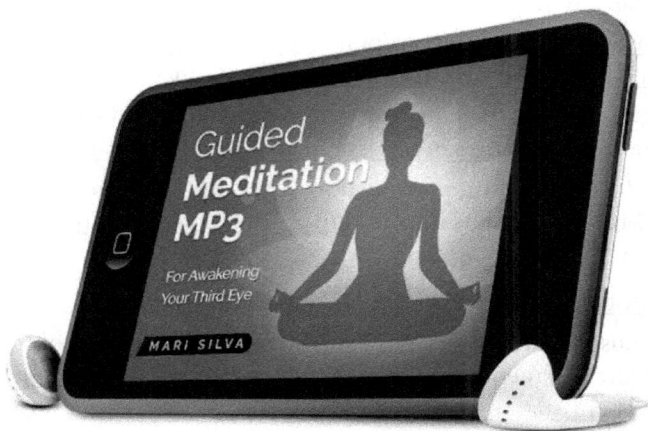

https://spiritualityspot.com/meditation

References

Goodrick-Clarke, N. (2008). Rosicrucianism. In The Western Esoteric Traditions (pp. 107–130). Oxford University Press.

Gordon Melton, J. (2020). Rosicrucian. In Encyclopedia Britannica.

Kameleon. (n.d.). A short history and introduction to the Rosicrucians. Pangeaproductions.Org.

Rosicrucians. (n.d.). Encyclopedia.Com. Retrieved from https://www.encyclopedia.com/philosophy-and-religion/other-religious-beliefs-and-general-terms/miscellaneous-religion/rosicrucians

The origins of Rosicrucianism. (2020, August 8). The Great Courses Daily. https://www.thegreatcoursesdaily.com/the-origins-of-rosicrucianism

What is Rosicrucianism, introduction in various languages and Dialects. (n.d.). AMORC. Retrieved from https://www.amorc.org/rosicrucianism

Alec nevala-lee. (n.d.). Alec Nevala-Lee. Retrieved from https://nevalalee.wordpress.com/tag/christian-rosenkreuz/

Anonymous, & Andreae, J. V. (2014). Chymical Wedding of Christian Rosenkreutz. Lulu.com. https://www.gohd.com.sg/shop/the-chymical-wedding-of-christian-rosenkreutz

Christian Rosenkreuz Explained. (n.d.). Explained.Today. Retrieved from https://everything.explained.today/Christian_Rosenkreuz

Christian_rosenkreuz. (n.d.). Chemeurope.Com. Retrieved from https://www.chemeurope.com/en/encyclopedia/Christian_Rosenkreuz.html

Westcott, W. W. (n.d.). Christian Rosenkreuz and the Rosicrucians. Website-Editor.Net. Retrieved from https://cdn.website-editor.net/e4d6563c50794969b714ab70457d9761/files/uploaded/Siftings_V6_A15a.pdf

Ebeling, F. (2007). The secret history of Hermes trismegistus: Hermeticism from ancient to modern times (D. Lorton, Trans.). Cornell University Press.

Empyreance IX - mysteries of Hermes the divine - learn online. (n.d.). Drdemartini.Com. Retrieved from https://drdemartini.com/learn/course/44/empyreance-ix-mysteries-of-hermes-the-divine

Hermes Trismegistos: Erkenntnis der Natur und des sich darin offenbarenden grossen Gottes. Begriffen in 17 unterschiedlichen Büchern nach griechischen und lateinischen Exemplaren in die Hochdeutsche übersetzt. (1997). EDIS.

Product details. (2019, April 2). Cornell University Press. https://www.cornellpress.cornell.edu/book/9780801445460/the-secret-history-of-hermes-trismegistus

The secret history of Hermes Trismegistus: hermeticism from ancient to modern times. (2008). Choice (Chicago, Ill.), 45(05), 45-2549-45-2549. https://doi.org/10.5860/choice.45-2549

Poimandres - Hermetica. (n.d.). Stjohnsem.Edu. Retrieved from http://ldysinger.stjohnsem.edu/@texts/0301_corp_herm/01_poimandres.htm

Poimandres—corpus hermeticum I. (n.d.). Themathesontrust.Org. Retrieved from https://www.themathesontrust.org/library/poimandres-corpus-hermeticum-i

The corpus hermeticum: I. poemandres, the Shepherd of Men. (n.d.). Gnosis.Org. Retrieved from http://gnosis.org/library/hermes1.html

Halperin, D. J. (n.d.). Descenders to the merkavah. Full-Stop.Net. Retrieved from https://www.full-stop.net/2020/06/25/blog/davidjhalperin/descenders-to-the-merkavah

Merkabah Mysticism or Ma'aseh Merkavah. (n.d.). Encyclopedia.Com. Retrieved from https://www.encyclopedia.com/religion/encyclopedias-almanacs-transcripts-and-maps/merkabah-mysticism-or-maaseh-merkavah

Merkavah Mysticism. (n.d.). Encyclopedia.Com. Retrieved from https://www.encyclopedia.com/environment/encyclopedias-almanacs-transcripts-and-maps/merkavah-mysticism

Robinson, G. (2002, November 15). Merkavah mysticism: The chariot and the chamber. My Jewish Learning. https://www.myjewishlearning.com/article/merkavah-mysticism-the-chariot-and-the-chamber

The Editors of Encyclopedia Britannica. (2020). Merkava. In Encyclopedia Britannica.

Avad_S. (2017, November 11). Sefirot/Emanations, Kabbalah. Sanctum Of Magick | Aminoapps.Com. https://aminoapps.com/c/sanctumofmagick/page/blog/sefirot-emanations-kabbalah/bN4v_bGDhou0MbKgw2ENqLWoZx3vqYd7dNK

Kabbalah and Healing :: Teachings :: Tree of life. (n.d.). Kabbalahandhealing.Com. Retrieved from http://www.kabbalahandhealing.com/tree-of-life.html

The Emanations — angelarium: The Encyclopedia of Angels. (n.d.). Angelarium: The Encyclopedia of Angels. Retrieved from https://www.angelarium.net/treeoflife

Are alchemy and kabbalah related? (n.d.). Quora. Retrieved from https://www.quora.com/Are-alchemy-and-kabbalah-related

Avad_S. (2017, November 11). Sefirot/Emanations, Kabbalah. Sanctum Of Magick | Aminoapps.Com. https://aminoapps.com/c/sanctumofmagick/page/blog/sefirot-emanations-kabbalah/bN4v_bGDhou0MbKgw2ENqLWoZx3vqYd7dNK

Bos, G. (n.d.). I:Iayyim vital's "practical kabbalah and alchemy": A 17th century book of secrets. Brill.Com. Retrieved from https://brill.com/previewpdf/journals/jjtp/4/1/article-p55_4.xml

Kabbalah and Healing :: Teachings :: Tree of life. (n.d.). Kabbalahandhealing.Com. Retrieved from http://www.kabbalahandhealing.com/tree-of-life.html

Ottmann, K. (n.d.). Alchemy and kabbalah : Scholem, Gershom Gerhard, Ottmann, Klaus: Amazon.In: Books. Amazon.In. Retrieved from https://www.amazon.in/Alchemy-Kabbalah-Gershom-Gerhard-Scholem/dp/0882145665

Sefirot - tree of Life. (n.d.). Geneseo.Edu. Retrieved from https://www.geneseo.edu/yoga/sefirot-tree-life

The Emanations — angelarium: The Encyclopedia of Angels. (n.d.). Angelarium: The Encyclopedia of Angels. Retrieved from https://www.angelarium.net/treeoflife

Atkinson, W. W. (2017). The secret doctrines of the Rosicrucians - E-book - William Walker Atkinson - storytel. Musaicum Books.

Holt, D. (2018, May 5). How to practice rosicrucianism. Phoenix Esoteric Society. https://phoenixesotericsociety.com/how-to-practice-rosicrucianism

On the practical paths of rosicrucianism. (n.d.). Futureconscience.Com. Retrieved from https://www.futureconscience.com/the-practical-paths-of-rosicrucianism

Rosicrucians. (n.d.). Encyclopedia.Com. Retrieved from https://www.encyclopedia.com/philosophy-and-religion/other-religious-beliefs-and-general-terms/miscellaneous-religion/rosicrucians

The origins of rosicrucianism. (2020, August 8). The Great Courses Daily. https://www.thegreatcoursesdaily.com/the-origins-of-rosicrucianism

Acher, F. (2020, October 10). Rosicrucian Magic. A manifest. Theomagica. https://theomagica.com/blog/rosicrucian-magic-a-manifest

Amorc, O. (2020, February 1). Three daily Rosicrucian practices to boost your energy, health, and happiness. Rosicrucians In Oregon. https://rosicruciansinportlandoregonwilsonville.com/2020/02/01/three-daily-rosicrucian-practices-to-boost-you-energy-health-and-happiness

Armstrong, S. (n.d.). daily routine – Podcasts. Rosicrucian.Org. Retrieved from https://www.rosicrucian.org/podcast/tag/daily-routine

Rosicrucian code of life. (n.d.). The Rosicrucian Order, AMORC. Retrieved from https://www.rosicrucian.org/rosicrucian-code-of-life

Rosicrucians. (n.d.). Encyclopedia.Com. Retrieved from https://www.encyclopedia.com/philosophy-and-religion/other-religious-beliefs-and-general-terms/miscellaneous-religion/rosicrucians

The origins of rosicrucianism. (2020, August 8). The Great Courses Daily. https://www.thegreatcoursesdaily.com/the-origins-of-rosicrucianism

17th Century Anon. (2011a). Secret symbols of the rosicrucians. Lulu.com. https://www.rosicrucian.org/secret-symbols-of-the-rosicrucians

17th Century Anon. (2011b). Secret symbols of the rosicrucians. Lulu.com. http://www.levity.com/alchemy/secret_s.html

Franz Hartmann - The Secret Signs of the Rosicrucians. (2015, August 2). HERMETICS. https://www.hermetics.net/media-library/rosicrucianism/franz-hartmann-the-secret-signs-of-the-rosicrucians/

(N.d.). Bookshop.Org. Retrieved from

https://bookshop.org/books/rosicrucian-rules-secret-signs-codes-and-symbols-esoteric-classics/9781631184888

Become a Member. (2006). IEEE Transactions on Mobile Computing, 5(5), 608–608. https://doi.org/10.1109/tmc.2006.56

Become a Rosicrucian Student. (n.d.). The Rosicrucian Order, AMORC. Retrieved from https://www.rosicrucian.org/become-a-student

Gordon Melton, J. (2020). Rosicrucian. In Encyclopedia Britannica.

How do you join the Rosicrucians? And how can you tell if your being recruited? (n.d.). Quora. Retrieved from https://www.quora.com/How-do-you-join-the-Rosicrucians-And-how-can-you-tell-if-your-being-recruited

Antoine Court de Gebelin. (n.d.). Stringfixer.Com. https://stringfixer.com/tr/Antoine_Court_de_Gebelin

ARTE. (n.d.). Les mystères du tarot de Marseille. ARTE Boutique – Films et séries en VOD, DVD, location VOD, documentaires, spectacles, Blu-ray, livres et BD. https://boutique.arte.tv/detail/mysteres_tarot_marseille

Bryce, C. (2021, May 20). What are the origins of tarot? Esri. https://storymaps.arcgis.com/stories/4732a3f9fd9c4bcc94d79d2dea1c1cdb

Classification, O. (n.d.). The international playing-card society PATTERN SHEET suit system IT. I-p-c-s.Org. https://i-p-c-s.org/pattern/PS002.pdf

Free Tarot Reading: Begin your journey. (n.d.). 7Tarot.Com. https://www.7tarot.com

Jean-Baptiste Alliette –. (n.d.). Tarot Heritage. https://tarot-heritage.com/tag/jean-baptiste-alliette

Origins of the tarot of Marseille – purple MAGAZINE. (2011, May 10). Purple. https://purple.fr/magazine/fw-2009-issue-12/origins-of-the-tarot-of-marseille

Parlett, D. (2009). tarot. In Encyclopedia Britannica.

Rider Waite Tarot Decks. (n.d.). Rider Waite Tarot Decks. https://riderwaitetarotdecks.com

Tarocchino Milanese. (n.d.). I-p-c-s.Org. https://i-p-c-s.org/pattern/ps-5.html

Tarot -- Philippe Camoin and the rebuilding of Tarot -- camoin Tarot de Marseille (Tarot of Marseilles). (n.d.). Camoin.Com. https://en.camoin.com/tarot/-Philippe-Camoin-Tarot-Restoration-en-.html

Tarot de Besançon. (n.d.). I-p-c-s.Org. https://i-p-c-s.org/pattern/ps-6.html

Tarot mythology: The surprising origins of the world's most misunderstood cards. (n.d.). Collectors Weekly. https://www.collectorsweekly.com/articles/the-surprising-origins-of-tarot-most-misunderstood-cards

Tarot mythology: The surprising origins of the world's most misunderstood cards. (2015, December 4). Mentalfloss.Com. https://www.mentalfloss.com/article/71927/tarot-mythology-surprising-origins-worlds-most-misunderstood-cards

Tarot of Marseille Heritage. (n.d.). Tarot of Marseille Heritage – Historic Tarots gallery. Tarot-de-Marseille-Heritage.Com. https://tarot-de-marseille-heritage.com/english/historic_tarots_gallery.html

The spellbinding history of tarot cards, from a mainstream card game to a magical ritual. (2020, April 19). My Modern Met. https://mymodernmet.com/history-of-tarot-cards

Visconti-Sforza tarot cards. (2015, September 9). The Morgan Library & Museum. https://www.themorgan.org/collection/tarot-cards

Visconti-Sforza Tarot deck. (n.d.). Tarot.Com. https://www.tarot.com/tarot/decks/visconti

Waite, E. A. (1993). Rider Waite Tarot Deck. Rider.

Wigington, P. (n.d.). A brief history of Tarot. Learn Religions. https://www.learnreligions.com/a-brief-history-of-tarot-2562770

Aleph – the power of the fool on the path from emanation to expansion. (2018, August 1). Mystical Breath. https://mysticalbreath.com/aleph-hebrew-alphabet

auntietarot. (2016, June 19). The Qabalah & the tarot. Auntietarot. https://auntietarot.wordpress.com/2016/06/19/the-qabalah-the-tarot

Divination: It's more Jewish than you think. (n.d.). Jewish Women's Archive. https://jwa.org/blog/divination-its-more-jewish-you-think

Giles, C. (2021, June 23). Kabbalah and Tarot: The tree of Life. Perspectives on Tarot. https://medium.com/tarot-a-textual-project/kabbalah-and-tarot-the-tree-of-life-ef0c170390c9

Hebrew letter Tarot correlations. (n.d.). Tarotforum.Net. https://www.tarotforum.net/showthread.php?t=21452

Huets, J. (2021, February 19). The Kabbalah and the Occult Tarot, part II. JEAN HUETS. https://jeanhuets.com/kabbalah-and-occult-tarot-part-2

Kabbalah, tarot, and delving into mystical Judaism. (n.d.). Reform Judaism. https://reformjudaism.org/blog/kabbalah-tarot-and-delving-mystical-judaism

Kabbalistic tarot: Hebraic wisdom in the major and minor Arcana (paperback). (n.d.). Rjjulia.Com. https://www.rjjulia.com/book/9781594770647

Kliegman, I. (1997). Tarot and the tree of life: Finding everyday wisdom in the minor Arcana. Quest Books.

Krafchow, D. (2005). Kabbalistic tarot: Hebraic wisdom in the major and minor Arcana. Inner Traditions International.

Laterman, K. (2021, January 29). How a kabbalistic tarot card reader spends his Sundays. The New York Times. https://www.nytimes.com/2021/01/29/nyregion/coronavirus-nyc-tarot-kabbalah.html

Merkabah. (n.d.). Newworldencyclopedia.Org. https://www.newworldencyclopedia.org/entry/Merkabah

My Jewish Learning. (2003, February 10). Kabbalah and mysticism 101. My Jewish Learning. https://www.myjewishlearning.com/article/kabbalah-mysticism-101

Oracle, D. ˜. A. (2017, February 26). The Shekinah. Archangel Oracle. https://archangeloracle.com/2017/02/26/the-shekinah

Robinson, G. (2002, November 15). Merkavah mysticism: The chariot and the chamber. My Jewish Learning. https://www.myjewishlearning.com/article/merkavah-mysticism-the-chariot-and-the-chamber

Sarkozi, C. (2021, February 18). The surprising connection between Torah and tarot. Alma. https://www.heyalma.com/the-surprising-connection-between-torah-and-tarot

Shekinah (La Papess) Beth-Moon. (n.d.). Tarotforum.Net. https://www.tarotforum.net/showthread.php?t=36612

The tarot and the Tree of life correspondences. (2020, July 8). Labyrinthos. https://labyrinthos.co/blogs/learn-tarot-with-labyrinthos-academy/the-tarot-and-the-tree-of-life-correspondences

The tree of Life and tarot. (2012, September 20). Truly Teach Me Tarot. https://teachmetarot.com/part-iii-major-arcana/the-kabbalah/the-sephiroth

Valente, J. (2017, May 8). The (sort of) secret kabbalah history in tarot. Luna Magazine. http://webcache.googleusercontent.com/search?q=cache:K1JGtWtWPRMJ:www.lunalunamagazine.com/dark/the-sort-of-secret-kabbalah-history-in-tarot+&cd=6&hl=en&ct=clnk&gl=tr

Weor, S. A. (2010). Tarot & kabbalah: The path of initiation in the sacred Arcana. Glorian Publishing.

What is Kabbalah? (2014). In Kabbalah : A Guide for The Perplexed. Continuum.

What is the Jewish opinion on the use of tarot cards and fortune-telling? (n.d.). Timesofisrael.Com. https://jewishweek.timesofisrael.com/what-is-the-jewish-opinion-on-the-use-of-tarot-cards-and-fortune-telling

Z. (2021, August 23). The Jewish history of tarot. Jewitches. https://www.jewitches.com/post/is-tarot-jewish

Hammer, R. J. (2021, November 8). Sefer Yetzirah: The Book of Creation. My Jewish Learning. https://www.myjewishlearning.com/article/sefer-yetzirah-the-book-of-creation

Ratzabi, H. (2002, November 15). The Zohar. My Jewish Learning. https://www.myjewishlearning.com/article/the-zohar

Liben, R. D., & JewishBoston. (2013, April 2). What is counting the omer? How can I participate? JewishBoston. https://www.jewishboston.com/read/what-is-counting-the-omer-how-can-i-participate

Jacobs, R. J. (2007, March 29). How to Count the Omer. My Jewish Learning. https://www.myjewishlearning.com/article/how-to-count-the-omer

The Middle Pillar. (n.d.). Webofqabalah.Com. https://www.webofqabalah.com/id25.html

The Qabalistic Cross. (n.d.). Webofqabalah.Com. https://www.webofqabalah.com/id24.html

Erdstein, B. E. (2010, November 1). Up at Midnight. Chabad.Org.

Vernon, J. (2016, September 12). Introduction to tarot and qabalah: Chesed and the tarot fours. Joy Vernon Astrology * Tarot * Reiki. https://joyvernon.com/introduction-to-tarot-and-qabalah-chesed-and-the-tarot-fours

The Tree of Life – Netzach – kabbalah and the sephirot. (2018, November 27). City Tarot. https://www.citytarot.com/netzach/

Hopler, W. (n.d.). What are the divine names on the Kabbalah Tree of Life? Learn Religions. https://www.learnreligions.com/divine-names-kabbalah-tree-of-life-124389

The contemplative life. (n.d.). The Contemplative Life.

Hopler, W. (n.d.-b). Who are the angels on the Kabbalah Tree of Life? Learn Religions. https://www.learnreligions.com/angels-kabbalah-tree-of-life-124294

The Tarot and the Tree of Life Correspondences. (2020, July 8). Labyrinthos. https://labyrinthos.co/blogs/learn-tarot-with-labyrinthos-academy/the-tarot-and-the-tree-of-life-correspondences

Kabbalah & The Tarot – learn the connection between Tarot & Kabbalah. (2018, November 8). City Tarot. https://www.citytarot.com/kabbalah-tarot-major-arcana

The Tree of Life and Tarot. (2012, September 20). Truly Teach Me Tarot. https://teachmetarot.com/part-iii-major-arcana/the-kabbalah/the-sephiroth

The Fool Meaning – Major Arcana Tarot Card Meanings. (2017, March 6). Labyrinthos. https://labyrinthos.co/blogs/tarot-card-meanings-list/the-fool-meaning-major-arcana-tarot-card-meanings

The Fool — Major Arcana Card. (n.d.). Sunnyray.Org. https://www.sunnyray.org/The-fool.htm

The Magician Meaning – Major Arcana Tarot Card Meanings. (2017, March 6). Labyrinthos. https://labyrinthos.co/blogs/tarot-card-meanings-list/the-magician-meaning-major-arcana-tarot-card-meanings

The Magician Tarot Card Meaning and Interpretation. (n.d.). Kasamba.Com. https://www.kasamba.com/tarot-reading/decks/major-arcana/the-magician-card

The High Priestess Meaning – Major Arcana Tarot Card Meanings. (2017, March 6). Labyrinthos. https://labyrinthos.co/blogs/tarot-card-meanings-list/the-high-priestess-meaning-major-arcana-tarot-card-meanings

The High Priestess Tarot Card Meaning and Interpretation. (n.d.). Kasamba.Com. https://www.kasamba.com/tarot-reading/decks/major-arcana/the-high-priestess-card

The Empress Meaning – Major Arcana Tarot Card Meanings. (2017, March 6). Labyrinthos. https://labyrinthos.co/blogs/tarot-card-meanings-list/the-empress-meaning-major-arcana-tarot-card-meanings

The Empress Tarot Card Meaning & Reverse Definition. (n.d.). Kasamba.Com. https://www.kasamba.com/tarot-reading/decks/major-arcana/the-empress-card

The Emperor Meaning – Major Arcana Tarot Card Meanings. (2017, March 6). Labyrinthos. https://labyrinthos.co/blogs/tarot-card-meanings-list/the-emperor-meaning-major-arcana-tarot-card-meanings

Reader, I. F. a. K. (n.d.). The Emperor Tarot Card Detailed Meaning. Kasamba.Com.

https://www.kasamba.com/tarot-reading/decks/major-arcana/the-emperor-card

The Hierophant Meaning – Major Arcana Tarot Card Meanings. (2017, March 7). Labyrinthos. https://labyrinthos.co/blogs/tarot-card-meanings-list/the-hierophant-meaning-major-arcana-tarot-card-meanings

The Hierophant Tarot Card. (n.d.). Sunnyray.Org. https://www.sunnyray.org/The-hierophant.htm

The Lovers Meaning – Major Arcana Tarot Card Meanings. (2017, March 7). Labyrinthos. https://labyrinthos.co/blogs/tarot-card-meanings-list/the-lovers-meaning-major-arcana-tarot-card-meanings

Reader, I. F. a. K. (n.d.). The Lovers Tarot Card Interpretation & Meaning. Kasamba.Com. https://www.kasamba.com/tarot-reading/decks/major-arcana/the-lovers-card

The Chariot Meaning – Major Arcana Tarot Card Meanings. (2017, March 7). Labyrinthos. https://labyrinthos.co/blogs/tarot-card-meanings-list/the-chariot-meaning-major-arcana-tarot-card-meanings

The Meaning of the Chariot Major Arcana. (n.d.). Sunnyray.Org. Retrieved.from

https://www.sunnyray.org/The-chariot.htm

Strength Meaning – Major Arcana Tarot Card Meanings. (2017, March 7). Labyrinthos. https://labyrinthos.co/blogs/tarot-card-meanings-list/strength-meaning-major-arcana-tarot-card-meanings

The Meaning and Symbolism of Strength Tarot Card. (n.d.). Sunnyray.Org.

https://www.sunnyray.org/Meaning-and-symbolism-of-strength-tarot-card.htm

The Hermit Meaning – Major Arcana Tarot Card Meanings. (2017, March 7). Labyrinthos. https://labyrinthos.co/blogs/tarot-card-meanings-list/the-hermit-meaning-major-arcana-tarot-card-meanings

The Hermit – Major Arcana 9. (n.d.). Sunnyray.Org. https://www.sunnyray.org/The-hermit-major-arcana-9.htm

The Wheel of Fortune Meaning – Major Arcana Tarot Card Meanings. (2017, March 7). Labyrinthos. https://labyrinthos.co/blogs/tarot-card-meanings-list/the-wheel-of-fortune-meaning-major-arcana-tarot-card-meanings

Wheel of Fortune – Meanings and Symbolism. (n.d.). Sunnyray.Org. https://www.sunnyray.org/Wheel-of-fortune.htm

Justice Meaning – Major Arcana Tarot Card Meanings. (2017, March 7). Labyrinthos.

https://labyrinthos.co/blogs/tarot-card-meanings-list/justice-meaning-major-arcana-tarot-card-meanings

The Meaning of Justice: Positive and Negative Aspects of Justice Tarot Card. (n.d.). Sunnyray.Org. https://www.sunnyray.org/The-meaning-of-justice-tarot-card.htm

The Hanged Man Meaning – Major Arcana Tarot Card Meanings. (2017, March 7). Labyrinthos. https://labyrinthos.co/blogs/tarot-card-meanings-list/the-hanged-man-meaning-major-arcana-tarot-card-meanings

The Hanged Man: Major Arcana Card Number 12. (n.d.). Sunnyray.Org. https://www.sunnyray.org/The-hanged-man.htm

Death Meaning – Major Arcana Tarot Card Meanings. (2017, March 7). Labyrinthos. https://labyrinthos.co/blogs/tarot-card-meanings-list/death-meaning-major-arcana-tarot-card-meanings

Reader, I. F. a. K. (n.d.). The Death Tarot Card Meanings and Interpretations. Kasamba.Com. https://www.kasamba.com/tarot-reading/decks/major-arcana/the-death-card

Temperance Meaning – Major Arcana Tarot Card Meanings. (2017, March 10). Labyrinthos. https://labyrinthos.co/blogs/tarot-card-meanings-list/temperance-meaning-major-arcana-tarot-card-meanings

Temperance: Major Arcana Card number 14. (n.d.). Sunnyray.Org. https://www.sunnyray.org/Temperance.htm

The Devil Meaning – Major Arcana Tarot Card Meanings. (2017, March 10). Labyrinthos. https://labyrinthos.co/blogs/tarot-card-meanings-list/the-devil-meaning-major-arcana-tarot-card-meanings

Reader, I. F. a. K. (n.d.). The Devil Tarot Card Meanings and Interpretations. Kasamba.Com. https://www.kasamba.com/tarot-reading/decks/major-arcana/the-devil-card

The Tower Meaning – Major Arcana Tarot Card Meanings. (2017, March 10). Labyrinthos. https://labyrinthos.co/blogs/tarot-card-meanings-list/the-tower-meaning-major-arcana-tarot-card-meanings

The Star Meaning – Major Arcana Tarot Card Meanings. (2017, March 10). Labyrinthos. https://labyrinthos.co/blogs/tarot-card-meanings-list/the-star-meaning-major-arcana-tarot-card-meanings

The Star Tarot Card – Major Arcana 17. (n.d.). Sunnyray.Org. https://www.sunnyray.org/The-star-tarot-card.htm

The Moon Meaning – Major Arcana Tarot Card Meanings. (2017, March 10). Labyrinthos. https://labyrinthos.co/blogs/tarot-card-meanings-list/the-moon-meaning-major-arcana-tarot-card-meanings

The Moon Tarot Card: Meanings and Symbolism. (n.d.). Sunnyray.Org. https://www.sunnyray.org/The-moon-tarot-card.htm

The Sun Meaning – Major Arcana Tarot Card Meanings. (2017, March 10). Labyrinthos. https://labyrinthos.co/blogs/tarot-card-meanings-list/the-sun-meaning-major-arcana-tarot-card-meanings

The Meaning of the Sun – Major Arcana nr. 19. (n.d.). Sunnyray.Org. https://www.sunnyray.org/The-meaning-of-the-sun.htm

Judgement Meaning – Major Arcana Tarot Card Meanings. (2017, March 10). Labyrinthos. https://labyrinthos.co/blogs/tarot-card-meanings-list/judgement-meaning-major-arcana-tarot-card-meanings

The Judgment Tarot Card Meaning for love & more. (n.d.). Kasamba.Com. https://www.kasamba.com/tarot-reading/decks/major-arcana/the-judgment-card

The World Meaning – Major Arcana Tarot Card Meanings. (2017, March 10). Labyrinthos. https://labyrinthos.co/blogs/tarot-card-meanings-list/the-world-meaning-major-arcana-tarot-card-meanings

Major Arcana 21 – The World. (n.d.). Sunnyray.Org. https://www.sunnyray.org/Major-arcana-21-the-world.htm

List of Minor Arcana Tarot Cards & Their Meanings. (n.d.). Kasamba.Com. https://www.kasamba.com/tarot-reading/decks/minor-arcana

The Tarot and the Tree of Life Correspondences. (2020, July 8). Labyrinthos. https://labyrinthos.co/blogs/learn-tarot-with-labyrinthos-academy/the-tarot-and-the-tree-of-life-correspondences

Andren, K. (2016, January 24). Astrology & the mystical Kabbalah. Keplercollege.Org.

Berg, R. (2000). Kabbalistic astrology: And the meaning of our lives. Research Centre of Kabbalah.

Halevi, B. S. (2017). A Kabbalistic Universe. Kabbalah Society.

Halevi, Z. S., & Halevi, B. S. (1987). The anatomy of fate: Kabbalistic astrology. Weiser Books.

Planets and the sefirot. (n.d.). LibraryThing.Com. https://www.librarything.com/topic/10037

Stuckrad, K. von. (2016). Astrology. In A Companion to Science, Technology, and Medicine in Ancient Greece and Rome (pp. 114–129). John Wiley & Sons, Inc.

Team Jothishi. (2019, September 1). Kabbalistic astrology: Natal charts, zodiac signs, and more! Jothishi. https://jothishi.com/kabbalistic-astrology

Yetzir, S. (1990). Kabbalist rav berg. Research Centre of Kabbalah.

Tree of Life Tarot Spread. (2016, January 10). Tarot Explained. https://www.tarot-explained.com/spreads/tree-of-life-tarot-spread

iFate. (n.d.). The Tree of Life Tarot Spread. IFate.Com. https://www.ifate.com/tarot-spreads/arrow-of-love-tarot-spread.html

Regan, S. (2021, October 6). The Simplest Tarot "Spread" For Quick Insight Anytime You Need It. Mindbodygreen. https://www.mindbodygreen.com/articles/one-card-tarot

learntarot. (2019, August 22). How to Do a Three Card Spread Tarot Reading for Beginners. The Simple Tarot. https://thesimpletarot.com/three-card-spread-tarot-reading

The Celtic Cross Tarot Spread – Exploring the Classic 10 Card Tarot Spread. (2018, May 29). Labyrinthos. https://labyrinthos.co/blogs/learn-tarot-with-labyrinthos-academy/the-celtic-cross-tarot-spread-exploring-the-classic-10-card-tarot-spread